THE DESIGN COLLECTIVE

VOLUME 2

CHRISTMAS

INSPIRATIONS

CONTENTS

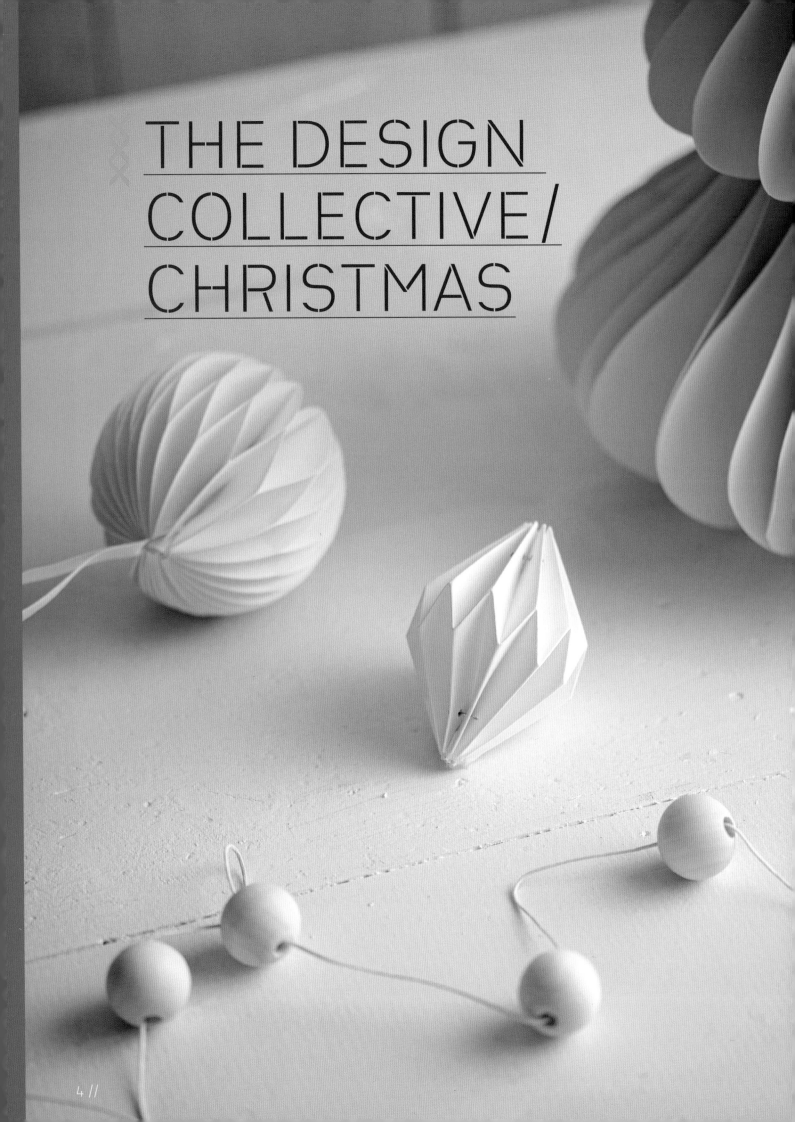

THE DESIGN COLLECTIVE/ CHRISTMAS

THE OBJECTIVE

Create a series of books to showcase the magnificent artistry of needlework and its ability to transform the ordinary into the extraordinary.

THE SUBJECT

Christmas. A story familiar to most.

With no room at the inn, baby Jesus is born to Mary and Joseph in a stable. He is wrapped in unassuming swaddling clothes and placed in a manger.

But as an Angel declared 'Today your Saviour was born in David's town, He is the Messiah, the Lord.' (Luke 2:11), shepherds and Wise Men alike flocked from afar to celebrate His birth.

Whilst the Magi celebrated with precious gifts of gold, frankincense and myrrh, today we celebrate this significant occasion with needle and thread.

THE APPROACH

Twelve of today's most accomplished and talented needlework artisans were invited to convey the spirit of Christmas in stitch.

Assigned the same brief and given total creative freedom, each designer was unencumbered by any criteria other than the fundamental requirement that the final piece must celebrate Christmas.

THE RESULTS

The creativity of a needlework artisan knows no bounds. While all twelve artists have indeed fulfilled the brief and brought forth projects in a unified celebration, the individual expression on display is wildly diverse, at times utterly unexpected, but always uplifting and wonderfully inspiring.

Across the board you will discover a joyous smattering of traditional motifs, including such delights as a nutcracker, hellebore (better known as the Christmas Rose), holly, poinsettia, snowflakes, fairy lights and even the Christmas star, that led the three wise men to Bethlehem.

The techniques demonstrated are perhaps a little more uniform with stumpwork and the creation of three-dimensional elements used to elevate and bring many of the designs to life.

Colour palettes centre around the classic hues of red, green, white and gold with a few projects dipping into the cooler colours of a sunny winter morning reflected in turquoise and soft pinks.

One of the big surprises is the diversity of finishes achieved. Where one might expect to see Christmas tree ornaments on high rotation, of which we are treated to some extraordinary examples, the parade of Christmas cheer extends far beyond this. You can look forward to a line-up of incredibly inventive, practical and truly inspired methods of both displaying and engaging with, stitched Christmas treasures.

Perhaps the most poignant aspect of the remarkable pieces these 12 artisans have crafted is the beautiful sentiments each convey. From a tribute to a dear friend who has passed, re-creating the magic of precious childhood memories on Christmas day, providing a receptacle to give messages of hope, through to the fashioning of generational heirlooms to enhance the gatherings of family and friends around a festive table, heartfelt and moving tributes abound.

IN SUMMARY

Each project is an invitation to join the designer on a journey of celebration and festivity. Be it ideas forged in reverence to the birth of a saviour, to the conviction of carrying forward family and cultural traditions, these designs embody not only a spiritual and emotional bond but also an embroidery connection.

These artisans are extraordinarily talented and highly skilled. The wonder and joy of the season is poetically reflected in the techniques chosen, the materials painstakingly selected and the final results.

There is no doubt, the significance of the season has well and truly been masterfully captured and majestically translated using needle and thread.

THE NUTCRACKER BY NATALIE DUPUIS

OVERVIEW

Designer: Natalie Dupuis	Project: Nutcracker	Technique: Or nué
Country of Origin: Canada	Fabric: Silk shantung	Threads: Metal threads, silk floss and paillettes
Dimensions: 15cm x 7cm wide (6" x 2¾")	Design Transfer Required: YES ☒ NO ☐	

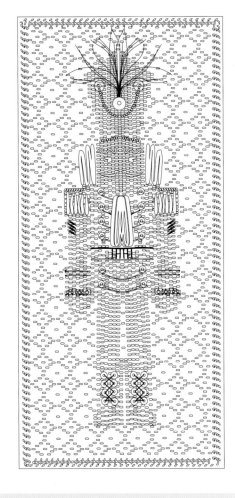

DESCRIPTION

Small panel suitable for framing or inserting in a box top featuring a traditional European nutcracker.

DESIGN NOTES

The nutcracker's association with Christmas began in 1892 with Tchaikovsky's famous, The Nutcracker ballet, set on Christmas Eve. In the Northern Hemisphere it has become a popular and colourful motif for festive decorations.

TECHNIQUE NOTES

Or nué, or shaded gold, is a beautiful thread technique where pairs of metal threads are couched to the fabric with silk or cotton, with the positioning and colour of the couching stitches forming the design. It was widely used for ecclesiastical embroidery in the Middle Ages and spectacular examples still exist in museums across Europe and North America. As an embroidery technique it is particularly suited to creating realistic effects with intricate shading.

Nutcrackers

In its most basic form, a nutcracker consists of two metal levers that are hinged at one end. The nut is placed between the levers, which are squeezed firmly, cracking the shell and revealing the edible interior. More decorative examples in the form of wooden carvings of soldiers, kings or knights date back to the 17th century and are thought to have originated in eastern Germany. These resemble a figure with a large mouth that opens by lifting a lever at the back of the figure. The nut is placed inside the mouth, the lever is pressed, closing the mouth and cracking the nut. In German folklore, these nutcrackers are thought to bring luck to the family, protect the home and represent power and strength, baring their teeth to chase away evil spirits. Contemporary examples often lack the original function but are a colourful and popular Christmas decoration in many parts of the world.

FROM THE
DESIGNER

"Designing a needlework piece with Christmas as the theme has to be the most squeal-with-excitement challenge I have ever accepted. I immediately thought of traditional motifs— poinsettia, red-breasted robin, colourful lights, St. Nicholas – and then progressed to thinking of a motif that would be interesting to stitch in or nué; the technique with which I am most comfortable.

I studied ballet in my youth and my daughter takes ballet classes. Every Christmas season there is excitement as we prepare to attend Les Grands Ballets Canadiens' production of The Nutcracker in Montreal. This link between Christmas and The Nutcracker ballet cemented the concept of designing an or nué nutcracker soldier or Nussknacker (nʊsˌknakɐ) as it is called in German.

I looked at hundreds of pictures of nutcracker soldiers and came up with a mix of shapes that seemed fun and suitable for or nué. I love the bright and playful colours from the costume of the nutcracker soldier used by Les Grands Ballet Canadiens. The primary colours recall festivity and a childlike simplicity, which is perfect for the holiday season. Thus, it was an easy design decision to use those colours when selecting silk threads.

I also greatly admire the creative embellishments that celebrated English embroiderer, Margaret Nicholson, is known to add to her finished or nué projects and wanted to pay tribute to her work by adding similar playful elements to Nussknacker. Nicholson was influential in the past century, but surface embellishment on or nué traces back to the 1400s with examples on the Golden Fleece vestments and many other notable extant embroideries.

Traditional or nué figures often have a diaper pattern in the background so this modern design includes one that uses bright neon blue as an accent."

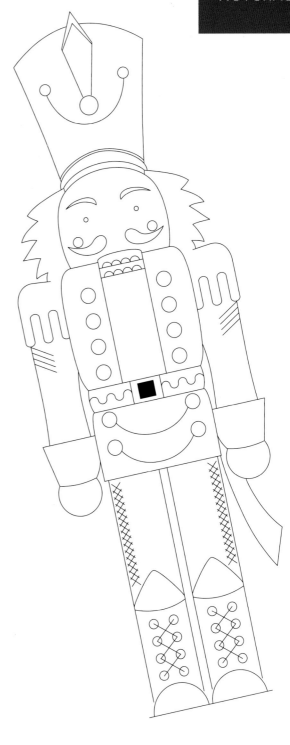

COLOUR PALETTE

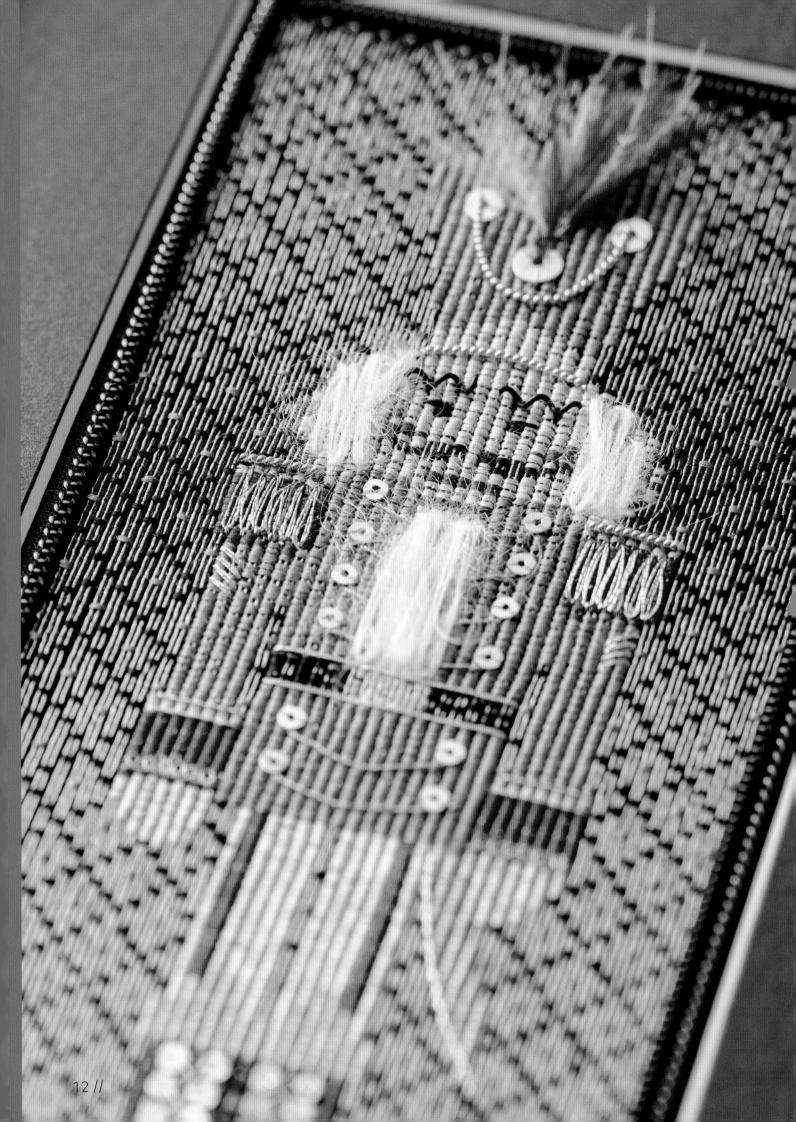

Fabric

30cm x 20cm wide (12" x 8")
piece of black silk shantung

40cm x 30cm wide (16" x 12")
piece of calico (muslin)

Supplies

Slate frame or stretcher bars
to fit calico

Lacing thread (slate frame)

Thumbtacks (stretcher bars)

20cm x 15cm wide (8" x 6")
piece of black wool felt

20cm x 15cm wide (8" x 6")
piece of mount board

Red, blue, yellow, beige,
grey and white coloured
pencils (optional)

Goldwork scissors

Mellor

Blunt-nose tweezers

Beeswax

Pair of koma or rolls of
wool felt

Tekobari or laying tool

Dressmaker's awl

Ruler

Set square

Silk pins

White ostrich feather

Red ostrich feather

Tissue paper

Fine black pen

Fine white gel pen

Needles

No. 18 chenille

No. 10 curved beading

No. 7 crewel

No. 10 crewel (10)

No. 12 crewel

Threads & paillettes

Golden Hinde *goldwork
translucent couching thread*
A = honey

Gütermann sewing thread
B = 000 black
C = 8 lt grey

Pipers Silks *silk floss*
D = neon blue
E = rust
F = brass
G = soft beige
H = black
I = deep slate
J = lt grey
K = stone
L = white

Rainbow Gallery Wisper
mohair/nylon thread
M = W88 white

Metal Threads

N = black smooth passing
no. 5 – 16m (17yd 24")

O = black pearl purl no. 2
– 50cm (20")

P = gilt super pearl purl
– 50cm (20")

Q = gilt Elizabethan twist
– 2m (2yd 8")

R = Japanese imitation gold
no. 1 – 5m (5yd 24")

S = Japanese imitation silver
twist no. 1 – 20cm (8")

Paillettes

T = 2mm gilt (28)
U = 4mm gilt (2)
V = 6mm gilt (1)

before you
begin

See the liftout pattern for the
embroidery design

We recommend that you read
the complete article

All embroidery is worked with
TWO strands of thread unless
specified

PREPARATION
FOR EMBROIDERY

Preparing the fabrics

Neaten the edges of the black silk with a machine
zigzag or overlock stitch to prevent fraying. Mount the
calico onto the frame, ensuring it is smooth and taut.
Centre the black silk over the calico and pin in place
with one pin at each corner and one along each side.
Using **C** in a no. 10 crewel needle and beginning at the
centre of one side, secure the silk to the calico using
long and short straight stitches worked perpendicular to
the edge of the silk. Work to one corner, making a stitch
every 5mm ($^3/_{16}$"). Return to the centre and work to the
opposite corner in the same manner (diag 1).

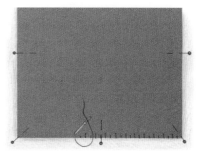

Repeat for the remaining sides. Remove the pins and
ensure the fabrics are drum tight.

Transferring the design

Using the black pen, trace the embroidery design and
placement marks onto the tissue paper. Centre the
tracing on the black silk, aligning the placement marks
with the straight grain, and hold firmly in place with the
silk pins. Using **C**, work very small back stitches over all
the design lines. Carefully tear away the tissue paper.
Use tweezers, if necessary, to remove all the paper. If
desired, colour the design using the coloured pencils
(fig 1).

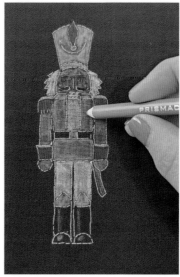

FIG 1

This will indicate the colour changes and cover the black silk background if the couched passing thread rows are a little far apart and the fabric is visible between the rows. Using the ruler and centering the figure, mark in a 14cm x 6.5cm (5½" x 2½") rectangle with the fine white gel pen (fig 2).

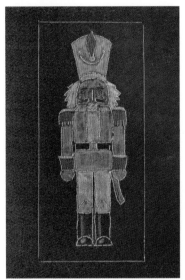

FIG 2

Using the set square and gel pen, mark in precise horizontal lines at 2.5mm (³⁄₃₂") increments down the design, working around the figure (fig 3).

FIG 3

Measure and mark an additional line at the upper and lower edges 1mm (¹⁄₃₂") out from the rectangle. These lines will be used when turning threads.

Measure and mark four, evenly spaced vertical lines down the rectangle, working over the design. These lines will help ensure that the couching remains parallel to the long edges of the rectangle.

Using **B** in a no. 10 crewel needle, work tiny pin stitches at 1cm (³⁄₈") intervals all over the design within the marked rectangle. This will anchor the layers of fabric together.

Preparing the passing thread

Wind 8m (8yd 2'3") of the black passing thread (**N**) onto each koma or felt roll. Tie the passing thread onto the koma and when winding the thread, turn the koma rather than the passing thread to help prevent the thread twisting or being pulled too taut.

EMBROIDERY

Refer to the close-up photograph for colour placement.

Use the no. 18 chenille needle for sinking the metal thread tails, the no. 7 crewel needle for the Elizabethan twist, the no. 10 crewels for couching and Japanese gold, the no. 12 crewel for the translucent couching thread and one strand of silk floss, and the no. 10 curved beading needle for securing the thread tails on the back of the work.

All embroidery is worked in a frame.

Order of work

COUCHING

Thread a single length of **B** into a no. 10 crewel needle and secure at the inner edge of the lower, left-hand corner on the marked turning line. Repeat at the upper, left-hand corner. These threads will remain at the short ends of the rectangle and will be used to turn the passing threads at the ends of the rows as the couching progresses.

Turn the frame 90 degrees counter-clockwise so that the long edges of the rectangle are at the top and base and the hat is at the left-hand side.

> **NOTE:** Before beginning the couching, look at the diaper pattern chart carefully so that you have a solid understanding of how it translates to the gridlines on the fabric. If you do not wish to use the diaper pattern, work the background couching in a brick pattern, offsetting the stitches in each row.

Thread one needle with **D** and a second needle with **H**.

Leaving 5cm (2") tails at the base of the design on the right-hand side, position two lengths of **N** along the lower edge of the rectangle. Begin couching the pair of threads using the colours as indicated. When working the first row, bring the needle to the front at an angle from beneath the outer edge of the passing threads and take it to the back at an angle beneath the inner edge (diag 2).

> **NOTE:** The black passing thread is delicate and easily damaged. Take care with each couching stitch not to nick the thread.

When reaching the end of the row, gently pull the passing threads to ensure they are taut and straight. If desired, carefully push the edge of the ruler against the row to straighten it.

Turning rows

Bring the length of **B** secured earlier to the front exactly on the turning line at the inner edge of the passing threads (a). Work a couching stitch over the passing threads (b). Make a small pin stitch to hold this couching stitch firmly in place. Bring the thread to the front again at the inner edge of the passing threads (a). Holding the thread firmly, turn the passing threads back across the rectangle.

> **HINT:** *Don't be afraid to strongly twist the threads around each other so that the passing forms a good bend. You will notice that the rounded part of the turn is slightly beyond the turning line.* **NATALIE**

Take the needle to the back on the turning line over the passing threads (c) (diag 3).

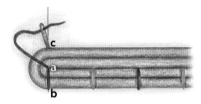

Work a small pin stitch to secure the couching stitch and complete the turn.

The couching for the second and subsequent rows is worked in the opposite direction to the first row. Bring the needle to the front at an angle from beneath the inner edge of the passing threads and take it to the back at an angle beneath previous row (diag 4).

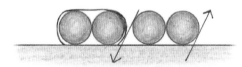

Couch the second row in the same manner as before, following the diaper pattern.

> **HINT:** Allow the pairs of passing threads to have tiny spaces between them, the width of the couching stitches, to prevent distorting the straight lines.

Turn the passing threads at the right-hand side in the same manner as before. Continue couching the passing thread in rows (fig 4).

Figure

When reaching the arm you will need to add in colours. Use a separate needle for each thread colour. Manage the multiple needles in a way that works for you, keeping the threads tightly stretched and out of the way until they are needed (fig 5).

Magnets placed along the upper edge of the frame can be used to hold needles when not in use.

Continue couching the passing threads in place, carefully following the design, until reaching the centre (fig 6).

> **NOTE:** It is up to you to decide how much of the passing thread you wish to cover with the coloured threads. The closer the couching stitches are placed, the denser the colour will be.

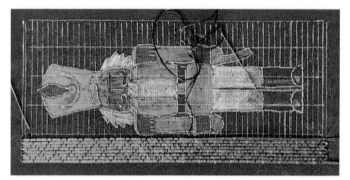

FIG 4

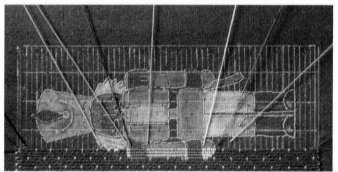

FIG 5

FIG 6

From the centre, you will need to carefully check the rows in the first half to ensure that the couching on the second half of the design is symmetrical. Depending on the row spacing, the stitching may need to be different to what the design lines indicate. Symmetry is more important than following the exact design lines (fig 7).

FIG 7

> **NOTE:** In the space between the legs and the body and the arms, take care to count the gridlines so that the diaper pattern is continued. Also take care when stitching the diaper pattern around the hat and boots to ensure that the pattern is correct.

Continue couching the passing threads in place until the design is complete. Once all embroidery is complete, sink the passing thread tails at the beginning and end of the design, one thread at a time. Secure the tails behind the couching using **B** and trim away the excess.

EMBELLISHMENTS

Use the photographs as a guide to placement.

Boots

Using one strand of **A** or **F**, attach eight, evenly spaced **T** paillettes to each boot, using two stitches for each one. Embroider the laces with straight stitch using **R**, working through the holes in the paillettes (fig 8).

FIG 8

Hat

Using one strand of **A** or **F**, attach two **U** and one **V** paillette at the marked positions (fig 9).

FIG 9

Stretch the length of **P** slightly. Cut a piece to fit along the lower edge of the visor and a piece to sit in a curve between the centres of the **U** paillettes. Couch each piece in place between the coils using **F**. Form a small bundle of red and white ostrich feathers and couch in place at the top of the **V** paillette with several stitches using **E** (fig 10).

FIG 10

Jacket

Cut and couch a length of **P** along the top of the epaulette on each shoulder using **F**. Using **R**, work six, long detached chains to complete the fringe. Using the same thread, work four, angled straight stitches over two rows of passing threads below each epaulette to form the rank stripes.

Using one strand of **A** or **F**, attach six, **T** paillettes down each side of the jacket (fig 11).

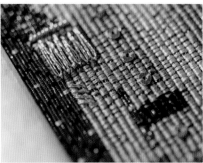

FIG 11

Thread a single strand of **Q** into the no. 7 crewel needle and work a curved straight stitch between the two paillettes at the lower edge of the jacket. Hold the curve in place by couching the stitch at the centre using one strand of **F**. Work a curved stitch between the remaining pairs of paillettes in the same manner.

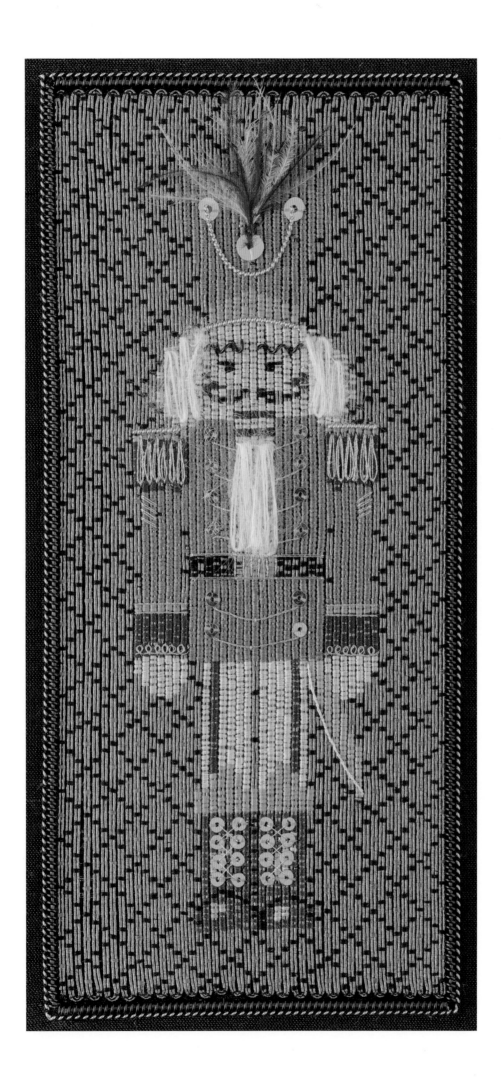

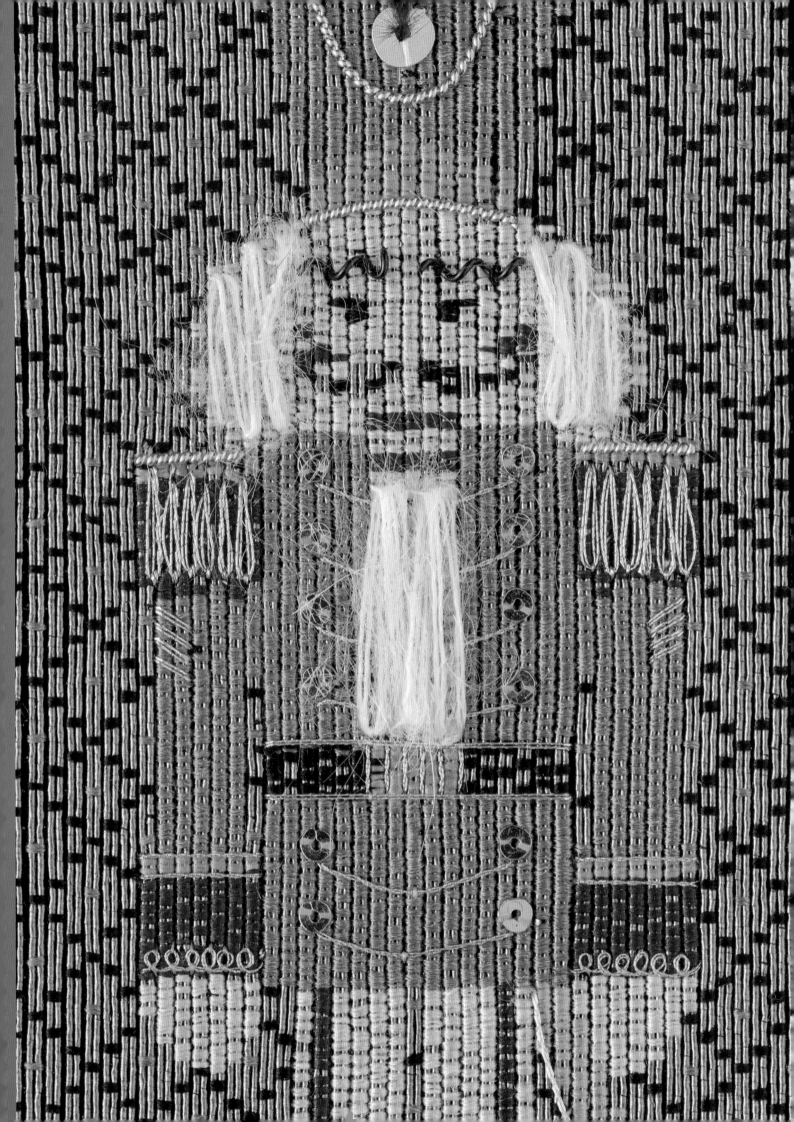

Outline each side of the belt with two, long straight stitches using one strand of **R**. Using one strand of **Q**, work a straight stitch down each side of the belt buckle and between each row of couching.

Embroider a straight stitch along each side of the yellow stripe at the top of the sleeve cuffs using **Q**. Using the same thread, work a series of loops along the lower edge of each cuff, holding the loops in place at the upper and lower edges using **A** (fig 12).

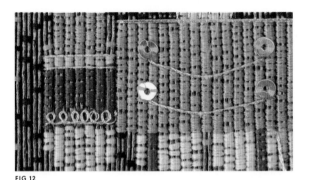

FIG 12

Beard

Secure a doubled strand of **L** at the base of the beard on the left-hand side. Cut a 1m (40") length of **M** and fold in half. Couch the fold at the base of the beard using **L** (fig 13).

FIG 13

Lay the lengths of **M** up along the beard and work a couching stitch over the thread at the upper point. Fold the lengths of **M** back down and couch in place at the base of the beard. Continue working in this manner until the beard is full. Stitch the hair on each side of the face in the same manner. Work a couching stitch at the centre of the innermost stitch on each side to hold it in a curve. Once all embroidery is complete, take the tails to the back and secure.

Eyebrows

Cut a 2cm (¾") length of **O** and stretch the desired amount. Cut two eyebrows from the length and couch in place using one strand of **H** (fig 14).

FIG 14

Sword

Leaving a 2cm (¾") tail at each end, couch a length of **S** along the inner edge of the sword using one strand of **J**. Once all embroidery is complete, sink the tails to the back, secure beneath the stitching using **A** and trim away the excess.

BORDER

Border 1

Cut ten, 30cm (12") lengths of **D**. Place in a bundle and wax heavily so that the strands stick together. Cut a 10cm (4") length of **O** and stretch to measure 16cm (6 ¼"). Trim away the unstretched ends. Wrap the length of **O** with the waxed lengths of **D**, leaving a minimum 5cm (2") tail of **D** at each end. Beginning at one corner, couch the length of **O** down one long side using one strand of **D**. When close to the end of the long side, carefully trim the pearl purl only to the correct length, unwinding the lengths of **D** if necessary. Complete the couching to the end of the line (fig 15).

FIG 15

Repeat on the remaining long side and both short sides of the rectangle, forming a neat join at each corner. Sink the tails of **D** at the corners, secure on the back of the work and trim away the excess.

Border 2

Cut two, 30cm (12") lengths of **H**. Place together and wax heavily so that the strands stick together. Cut a 10cm (4") length of **P** and stretch to measure 16cm (6¼"). Trim away the unstretched ends. Wrap the length of **P** with the waxed lengths of **H**, leaving a minimum 5cm (2") tail of **H** at each end. Beginning at one corner, couch the length of **P** down one long side, outside Border 1, using one strand of **H**. When close to the end of the long side, carefully trim the pearl purl only to the correct length, unwinding the lengths of **H** if necessary. Complete the couching to the end of the line.

Repeat on the remaining long side and both short sides of the rectangle, forming a neat join at each corner. Sink the tails of **H** at the corners, secure on the back of the work and trim away the excess.

FINISHING

Cut the piece of mount board and black wool felt to the required size. Position the felt over the mount board. Carefully centre the embroidery over the felt and pin the fabric in place around each side of the board. Fold a piece of tissue paper to cover and protect the embroidery while lacing and pin in place. Turn to the wrong side and lace the long sides of the fabric over the board, checking the positioning carefully and adjusting if necessary, before lacing the short sides. Take care to ensure that the surface is taut. Remove the pins. Place the embroidery in a box top or frame as desired.

A CHRISTMAS ROSE
BY BETSY MORGAN

OVERVIEW

Designer:	Project:	Technique:
Betsy Morgan	Hanging ornament with star and hellebore	Metal thread, counted thread and stumpwork
Country of Origin:	**Fabric:**	**Threads:**
USA	Linen	Stranded silk and metal thread

Dimensions:
10.5cm x 7cm wide (4⅛" x 2¾")

Design Transfer Required: YES ☒ NO ☐

DESCRIPTION

A hexagonal ornament featuring a pink hellebore combining counted thread, goldwork and stumpwork techniques.

DESIGN NOTES

The stumpwork sepals of the hellebore sit within a gilt pearl purl, six-pointed star outline and against an overall background design of leaves worked onto cream linen.

TECHNIQUE NOTES

Counted thread techniques require evenweave linen and a specified thread count should be used to replicate the original exactly. Gilt pearl purl is a metal thread that is cut to the exact size and couched to a base fabric with a waxed sewing thread while the stumpwork elements are stitched onto finely woven cotton fabric with a wired edge that allows them to be attached only at the base.

Hellebore

Commonly known as the Christmas, Lenten or winter rose, the Eurasian genus Helleborus is made up of around twenty species that occur naturally across Europe and China and flower from late autumn into winter. Not related at all to the rose, hellebores are part of the Ranunculaceae family, and many species are poisonous. Each single flower consists of five, showy sepals that surround a central ring of cup-shaped nectaries that are modified petals. Rather than falling away, the sepals remain on the plant for a long time and are thought to aid the development of the seeds that form in striking, spurred capsules. The plant also has attractive leaves and maintains a pleasing appearance for many months at a time when little else is flowering in the garden. From the original single flowers, multi-petalled hybrids have been developed in shades from pure white to almost black with some featuring spotting, striping and coloured margins.

FROM THE
DESIGNER

"This ornament was inspired by my favourite Christmas hymn, Lo How A Rose E'er
Blooming. The hymn is German in origin and has a lovely and unusual melody.
The Rose in the hymn is Christ and the words, e're blooming, refer to his being
eternal. The Christmas Rose is actually a hellebore and is one of my favourite
flowers. It comes in a wide variety of colours and is easy to grow. Rather than
include stumpwork leaves with the flower, I chose to use my favourite counted
thread technique to stitch the leaves in the background. The goldwork star,
echoing the Star of David, is an acknowledgment that Christianity is rooted in
Judaism and that Christ was a Jew. Having spent the last two decades designing
counted thread etuis, I wanted to do something different with this project. After
counted thread, stumpwork is my favourite needlework technique and I wanted
to include it. Though I am no expert at goldwork, I thought that it would be
another nice addition to this design and felt that it was appropriate for the star."

Lo how a rose e'er blooming
From tender stem hath sprung
Of Jesse's lineage coming
As seers of old have sung
It came a flower bright
Amid the cold of winter
When half spent was the night

Isaiah 'twas foretold it
The rose I have in mind
With Mary we behold it
The virgin mother kind
To show God's love aright
She bore to us a saviour
When half spent was the night

O flower whose fragrance tender
With sweetness fills the air
Dispel in glorious splendour
The darkness everywhere
True man yet very God
From sin and death now save us
And share our every load

COLOUR PALETTE

REQUIREMENTS

Fabric
20cm (8") square of cream
36-count linen

20cm (8") square of white
quilter's muslin

15cm x 10cm wide (6" x 4")
piece of light gold silk
dupion

Supplies
Stretcher bars to fit fabric or
15cm (6") embroidery hoop

Thumbtacks (stretcher bars)

12.5cm (5") embroidery hoop

10cm x 12.5cm wide (4" x 5")
piece of lightweight fusible
interfacing

15cm x 20cm wide (6" x 8")
piece of interlining

36cm (14") lengths of 33
gauge white paper-covered
wire (3)

4.5cm x 6cm wide (1¾" x
2⅜") piece of firm card

Fine sharp embroidery
scissors

Scissors to cut wire

Blunt-nose tweezers

Beeswax

Tracing paper

Fine black pen

Fine heat-soluble fabric
marker

Needles
No. 18 chenille
No. 9 crewel
No. 26 tapestry
No. 28 tapestry

Threads
Au ver à Soie, soie d'Alger
stranded silk
A = F1 cream
B = 236 dk Kelly green
C = 934 poppy
D = 2544 med corn

***DMC** no. 12 perlé cotton*
E = 676 lt old gold

***Gütermann** polyester
sewing thread*
F = 488 gold

Metal thread
G = gilt pearl purl no. 2
– 45cm (18")

this design uses

Back stitch, p214

Couching, p214

Double running stitch, p208

Blanket stitch, p214

French knot, p214

Ghiordes knot, p214

Joining stitch, p209

Long and short stitch, p215

Straight stitch, p215

before you begin

See the liftout pattern for the sepal template

We recommend that you read the complete article

All embroidery is worked with ONE strand of thread unless specified

-----

PREPARATION FOR EMBROIDERY

Preparing the fabrics

Neaten the edges of the linen and quilter's muslin with a machine zigzag or overlock stitch to prevent fraying.

Transferring the design

BACKGROUND EMBROIDERY

At the upper left-hand corner of the linen square measure in and mark 4.5cm (1¾") from the upper edge and 10cm (4") from the side edge. Beginning at this point, work lines of tacking using **F** and working over and under four threads to mark out the hexagon following the chart.

Mount the linen in the frame or 15cm (6") hoop, ensuring the grainlines remain straight and the surface is drum tight.

DETACHED SEPALS

Using the black pen, trace the sepal template onto tracing paper. Tape the tracing to a lightbox or window. Centre the inner ring of the 12.5cm (5") hoop onto the square of quilter's muslin. Using the heat-soluble fabric marker, trace around the inner edge of the ring to mark a circle. Working within the marked circle, transfer the shaping for five sepals using the heat-soluble marker. Place the fabric into the 12.5cm (5") hoop and tension until drum tight, taking care not to distort the shapes.

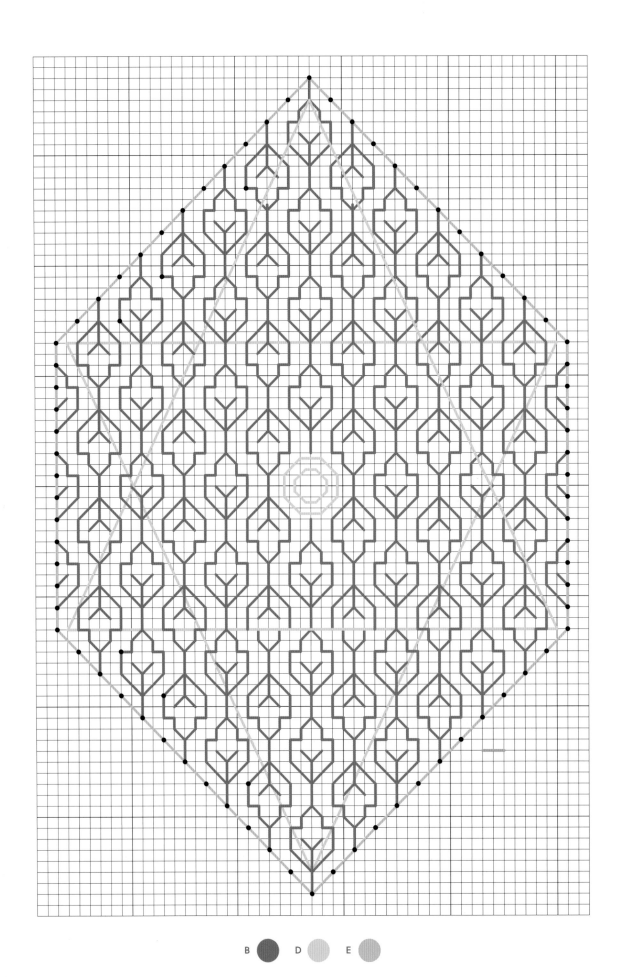

B ● D ● E ●

EMBROIDERY

Refer to the chart and close-up photograph for colour and stitch placement.

Use the no. 26 tapestry needle for the perlé cotton and the no. 28 tapestry for the double running stitch. Use the no. 18 chenille needle to sink wire tails and the no. 9 crewel needle for all other embroidery and construction.

All embroidery is worked in a frame and hoop.

Each square on the chart represents 2 x 2 fabric threads.

Order of work

All stitches are worked over two threads unless specified.

BACKGROUND EMBROIDERY

Leaves

Working in columns and using **B**, embroider the leaves and stems with double running stitch. Stitch the ornament outline with back stitch over four threads using **E**, removing the tacking as you work.

Preparing templates

Remove the linen from the frame or hoop and make two photocopies of the embroidered area. Cut out one copy, trimming away the back stitch borders, and label as the small template. Trim the remaining copy to the outer edge of the back stitch border and label as the large template.

Interfacing the linen

Using the small template, cut a piece of fusible interfacing and check that it fits inside the back stitch border on the wrong side of the embroidered linen. Trim if necessary and, with the embroidery face down into a soft, padded surface, fuse in place with an iron.

Place the linen back into the frame or hoop in the same manner as before.

Star

Cut **G** into two, 22.5cm (9") lengths. Holding each end of one length of the purl, gently stretch to slightly open out the coils and stiffen the purl. Trim away any unstretched purl at each end. Repeat for the remaining length. Referring to the chart, the triangle with the apex pointing upwards is outlined first. Position the end of one length at the upper point of the star. Using a waxed length of **F**, couch the first two coils in place along the first side of the triangle. Continue to couch the purl in the same manner after every third or fourth coil. At the first corner, carefully bend the purl using the tweezers and couch in place along the second side of the triangle in the same manner as before. Follow the step-by-step instructions for turning corners with pearl purl on page 213. Repeat at the next corner and third side of the triangle. When nearing the tip, trim the purl to the exact length for a neat finish and complete the couching to the triangle tip. Work a stitch between each of the last few coils.

Rotate the work 180 degrees and outline the second triangle using **G** and **F** in the same manner. Where the second triangle crosses the first, work a couching stitch at each side of the intersection.

Flower centre

Referring to the chart, fill the inner octagon with French knots using two strands of **D**. Using two strands of the same thread, outline the area of French knots with a row of Ghiordes knots, ensuring the loops are approximately 2cm (¾") long. Cut and trim the loops to 13mm (½") in length but do not comb or brush the thread tails.

PREPARING THE EMBROIDERED LINEN AND SILK

Remove the linen from the frame or hoop. Leaving a 13mm (½") seam allowance from the back stitch outline, cut out the embroidered hexagon. Using this piece as a template, cut a hexagon of silk for the ornament back.

Finger press the linen seam allowance to the wrong side, folding on the first linen thread outside the back stitch border. Using the small and large photocopy templates, cut one piece of interlining in each size. Label the smaller piece, linen, and the larger piece, silk. Set aside for construction.

DETACHED SEPALS

Cut five, 12cm (4¾") lengths of white paper-covered wire. Fold one length in half and position the wire with the fold at the tip of one sepal shape on the quilter's muslin. Using **A** and beginning at the tip, couch the wire in place along one side of the sepal outline, spacing the stitches 6mm (¼") apart. At the base of the sepal, bend the wire to form a tail. Repeat to couch the remaining half of the wire in place along the second half of the outline. At the base, work two couching stitches over both wire tails.

Using the same thread, work close blanket stitch over the wire. Fill the sepal with long and short stitch using **A**, beginning at the tip and angling the stitches towards the base. Referring to the close-up photograph, embroider the sepal markings with straight stitch using **C**, varying the length of each stitch and angling them towards the base. Work the remaining four sepals in the same manner.

CUTTING OUT AND ATTACHING THE SEPALS

Remove the embroidered sepals from the hoop and carefully cut out using the fine, sharp embroidery scissors and following the step-by-step instructions on page 207. Referring to the close-up photograph for placement, insert the wire tails of each petal at evenly spaced positions around the flower centre following the step-by-step instructions on page 212. Take care to fold the Ghiordes knots out of the way so that the thread tails are all to the inside of the sepals. Before securing and trimming the wire tails, check that you are happy with the position of each sepal. When securing the wires, take care to only stitch through the interfacing on the wrong side of the linen.

CONSTRUCTION

All seam allowances are 13mm (½"). The shaded areas on the following diagrams indicate the right side of the fabric.

Preparing the ornament front

With the wrong side facing up, open out the folded seams and insert the smaller piece of prepared interlining. Refold the seam allowance, hand stitch the corner folds and tack the seam allowance in place using **F** (diag 1).

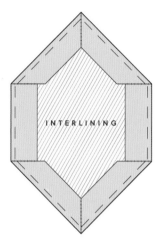

Preparing the ornament back

Centre the larger piece of prepared interlining over the wrong side of the silk dupion. Fold the seam allowance over the edges of the interlining and press. Hand stitch the corner folds and tack down the seam allowance in the same manner as the ornament front.

Twisted cords and tassel

Using four, 75cm (30") lengths of **E**, make a 25cm (10") twisted cord for the hanging loop. Bind the knotted end of the cord to secure and trim away the knots (diag 2).

Using four, 24cm (9½") lengths of **E**, make an 8cm (3⅛") twisted cord for the tassel. Using four, 70cm (27") lengths of **E**, make a 23cm (9") twisted cord for the tassel neck. Bind and trim the knotted end of the 8cm (3⅛") twisted cord in the same manner as the 25cm (10") cord.

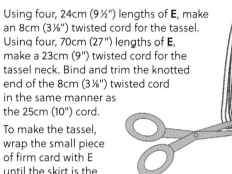

To make the tassel, wrap the small piece of firm card with E until the skirt is the desired fullness. Cut the thread bundle at the base (diag 3).

On a flat surface, centre the bundle over the 8cm (3⅛") cord. Carefully bring the ends of the cord together and bind or stitch so that the thread bundle lies over the base of the loop (diag 4).

Referring to the step-by-step instructions on page 206, wrap the 23cm (9") cord around the thread bundle to form the tassel neck. Trim the base of the skirt so that it is even.

Assembling the ornament

With wrong sides facing and using **F**, stitch the front and back together with joining stitch along one side, beginning one back stitch from the upper tip to 2–3 back stitches from the lower point. Insert approximately 13mm (½") of the joined ends of the tassel cord between the panels. Make several stitches back and forth through the cords and seam allowance to secure. Continue working joining stitch along the remaining side until one stitch from the tip. Insert approximately 13mm (½") of the two ends of the 25cm (10") cord between the panels. Secure the cords and panels at the tip in the same manner as at the lower point. Remove any remaining tacking.

Carefully adjust the sepals so that they curve gently upwards.

A SPRIG OF HOLLY BY SUSAN O'CONNOR

OVERVIEW

Designer:	Project:	Technique:
Susan O'Connor	Holly brooch	Three-dimensional embroidery
Country of Origin:	**Fabric:**	**Threads:**
Australia	Cotton poplin	Stranded silk

Dimensions:	Design Transfer Required: YES [X] NO [ ]
4.5cm x 7.5cm wide (1¾" x 3")	

DESCRIPTION

Spray of holly leaves and berries attached to a locking brooch pin.

DESIGN NOTES

A quintessential symbol of Christmas, the holly brooch is designed to be robust so that it can be attached to any suitable surface. Lustrous stranded silk is used for the stitching.

TECHNIQUE NOTES

Worked onto fine cotton poplin, the leaves are wired along the centre vein with overcasting and around the outer edge with blanket stitch, covered with stitching then cut out. Glass pebble beads are wrapped with thread and finished with a small bead and fine wire stem. Stems are wrapped together with thread then combined with the leaf stems to form a small branch that is stitched to a narrow brooch pin.

Holly

Holly (Ilex aquifolium) is a small, evergreen tree with glossy, dark-green leaves with spiny edges, fragrant white flowers in late spring to early summer and gleaming red berries in winter. The Romans believed holly had mystical qualities and used it as a decoration during their Saturnalia festival that was held in mid to late December. One of the most beloved trees in Celtic mythology, it was thought to control the dark, winter months and was considered sacred by the Druids who regarded it as a symbol of fertility and eternal life. Now utilised by Christians to celebrate Christmas, the sharp leaves are said to symbolise the crown of thorns worn by Christ and the red berries represent his blood.

FROM THE
DESIGNER

A SPRIG
OF HOLLY

"Many years ago, I bought my mother a holly brooch as a Christmas gift that, if I recall correctly, was inspired by the holly trees used prolifically in the 15th century Unicorn Tapestries that are on display at The Cloisters, the medieval branch of *The Metropolitan Museum of Art* in New York. I have always loved the brooch, the original carefully fashioned from beautifully patinated metal with red jade beads for the berries, and it is such a lovely, elegant symbol of the festive season while being a beautiful piece of jewellery. This seemed the perfect opportunity to create my own with embroidery and I wanted to try a three-dimensional piece using some of the stumpwork techniques that are now commonly used. The colours that I chose were influenced by the finish on the original brooch, with the golden tones of soft, grape greens rather than the usual harder, blue-based, dark greens of the holly plant. The berries had to be a wonderful, glowing red and it was hard to choose from the fabulous range that *Au Ver à Soie, soie d'Alger* silk thread offers but I decided on a lovely, warm garnet shade. The wires used to shape the leaves are a little thicker than would normally be used but this gives them stability and prevents them from becoming misshapen if knocked – important for something that is designed to be worn. Each leaf and berry is created separately then the ends of the leaf wires are wrapped to form the stem, with a small twig added at the end, just as in the original brooch."

COLOUR PALETTE

REQUIREMENTS

Fabric
15cm (6") square of ivory cotton poplin

Supplies
10cm (4") embroidery hoop

23cm (9") lengths of 24 gauge green paper-covered wire (5)

28 gauge gold beading wire – 30cm (12")

Fine sharp embroidery scissors

Scissors to cut wire

32mm (1 ¼") narrow locking gold brooch pin

Craft glue

Toothpick

Fine black pen

Tracing paper

Fine heat-soluble fabric marker

Needle
No. 10 sharp

Threads & Beads
Au Ver à soie, soie d'Alger
stranded silk
A = 944 med garnet
B = 2144 med grape green
C = 2145 dk grape green
D = 3733 lt khaki

Mill Hill pebble beads
E = 05025 ruby (3)

Toho size 11 seed beads
F = 46 opaque oxblood (3)

this design uses

Blanket stitch, p214

Long and short stitch, p215

Overcasting, p215

Wrapping

before you begin

See the liftout pattern for the leaf templates

We recommend that you read the complete article

All embroidery is worked with ONE strand of thread

PREPARATION FOR EMBROIDERY

Preparing the fabric

Neaten the edge of the poplin square with a machine zigzag or overlock stitch to prevent fraying.

Transferring the design

Using the black pen, transfer the leaf shaping onto tracing paper. Using a lightbox or window if necessary, transfer the shaping onto the poplin, taking care to ensure that all leaves will fit inside the hoop. Place the poplin in the hoop and tension until drum tight, taking care not to distort the leaf shaping.

EMBROIDERY

Refer to the close-up photograph for colour placement. All embroidery is worked in the hoop.

Order of work

LEAVES

Each leaf is worked in the same manner.

Cut a 5cm (2") length of green, paper-covered wire. Using **D**, couch the wire along the centre vein, beginning at the tip. Using the same thread, overcast the wire from the vein tip to the leaf base so that it is completely covered. There will be a small section of wire at the leaf base that is free of stitching. Bend a 23cm (9") length of green, paper-covered wire in half, pinching the fold with pliers if necessary to ensure that it is sharp. Beginning at the tip of the leaf with the fold and using **D**, couch one half of the wire down one side of the leaf then the other half down the second side, leaving a tail at each end. At the base of the leaf, the tails of wire should sit on each side of the end of the vein wire (diag 1).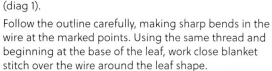

Follow the outline carefully, making sharp bends in the wire at the marked points. Using the same thread and beginning at the base of the leaf, work close blanket stitch over the wire around the leaf shape.

Fill the inner area of the leaf with long and short stitch using **C**, angling the stitches towards the tip. Using **B**, work the outer area in a similar manner, bringing the needle to the surface through the end of each existing stitch and taking it to the back over the wire and inside the beaded edge of the blanket stitch. Remove the fabric from the hoop and carefully cut out each leaf using the fine, sharp embroidery scissors, following the step-by-step instructions on page 207.

Secure a length of **B** on the wrong side at the base of the leaf. Carefully trim the end of the vein wire 2mm (1/16") from the base of the leaf. Push the wire end to the back and the two long wire tails together. Using the toothpick, coat approximately 5mm (3/16") of the wires with a thin layer of glue and wrap firmly for 5mm (3/16"). Secure with a half hitch and allow to dry. Do not trim away the thread.

> **NOTE:** Use the glue very sparingly as you only need just enough to hold the thread in place. Excess glue will be forced out between the wraps and will discolour and damage the thread. Use a damp cotton bud to remove any excess glue.

BERRIES

Leaving a 5cm (2") tail, tie a length of **A** onto one **E** bead. Adjust the thread so that the knot is inside the bead. Working down through the hole, wrap the bead until it is completely covered. Cut a 10cm (4") length of gold beading wire. Fold the wire in half and pinch the fold firmly. Take the wrapping thread between the wire tails then take the needle back up through the **E** bead, catching the threads in the hole. Pull the thread firmly so that the wire fold is pulled up into the hole. Thread an **F** bead onto the needle and take it back down through the **E** bead. Take the thread between the wire tails then take the needle back up through the **E** bead as before. Take the needle through the **F** bead then back down through the **E** bead. Tie the working thread and tail together at the base of the bead. Take each thread up through the **E** bead, pull firmly and trim very close to the bead. Secure a length of **B** at the base of the berry very close to the wire tails. Using the toothpick, coat approximately 5mm (3/16") of the wires with a thin layer of glue and wrap for 5mm (3/16"). Secure with a half hitch and allow to dry. Trim the wire tails to measure 2cm (3/4"). Do not trim away the thread.

Make two more berries in the same manner.

ASSEMBLING THE SPRIG

Joining the berries

Place two berry stems together, ensuring that the base of the wrapping on each one is touching the other. Apply a small dab of glue below the wrapping and, using one of the left wrapping threads, wrap the wires and thread twice. Trim away one wire on one stem and the unused left thread close to the wrapping. Add in the third berry and wrap the wires and threads twice. Trim away one wire and the thread of the third berry close to the wrapping. Add a little more glue to the wires and wrap for 3mm (1/8"). Secure the thread with a half hitch and allow to dry. Do not trim away the thread.

Attaching the leaves to the berries

Position the small leaf on the upper side of the berries, aligning the base of the wrapping, add a little more glue and wrap all wires for 3mm (1/8"). Position the large leaf, wrong side uppermost, on the lower side of the berries, aligning the base of the wrapping, add a little more glue if necessary and wrap all wires for 3mm (1/8"). Position the medium leaf between the previous leaves and wrap all wires for 3cm (1 1/4") adding glue as necessary. Secure the thread with a half hitch and leave to dry. Do not trim away the thread.

> **NOTE:** If it is necessary to join in a new wrapping thread, trim the tail of the old thread to 1cm (3/8") and glue it and 1cm (3/8") at the beginning of the new thread to the wires, adjacent to the end of the wrapping and facing down to the end of the wires (diag 2).
>
>
>
> Allow to dry. Continue wrapping with the new thread, working over the base of the previous wrapping once or twice to ensure that the join in invisible.

Trim all the wires so that they measure approximately 4cm (1 1/2") from the point that the medium leaf was added.

Small twig

Cut a 2cm (3/4") length of green, paper-covered wire. Wrap 5mm (3/16") at the centre of the wire using **B**. Secure the thread with a half hitch and leave. Fold the wire in half, pressing the halves together firmly to ensure there is no loop at the fold. Apply a little glue and wrap the wires back to the fold then back 5mm (3/16") down the doubled wire. Secure the thread with a half hitch and carefully cut away one wire tail. Bend the wrapped end of the twig back a little. Position the wire end of the twig at the base of the leaf wires, aligning the ends, apply a little glue and using the twig wrapping thread, wrap all unwrapped wires several times to secure the twig to the stem. Work a half hitch knot, add a small dab of glue to the knot and allow to dry. Trim away the thread. You should have one remaining wrapping thread attached close to the joining point of the twig (diag 3).

Cut six, 6mm (1/4") lengths of **B**. Apply a small amount of glue to the end of the wires and glue three of the lengths over the ends then the remaining three over the ends perpendicular to the first group (diag 4).

Using the remaining wrapping thread, wrap to the end of the stem, ensuring that all the wire is covered. Secure the wrapping thread with a half hitch knot and small dab of glue. Allow to dry and trim away the excess. Shape the stem into a gentle curve.

Finishing

Using the photograph as a guide, bend the small leaf so that it is perpendicular to the stem. Fold the large leaf back and using **B**, attach the edge to the stem. Using the same thread attach one end of the brooch back to the back of the medium leaf and the other end to the stem. Shape the leaves as desired.

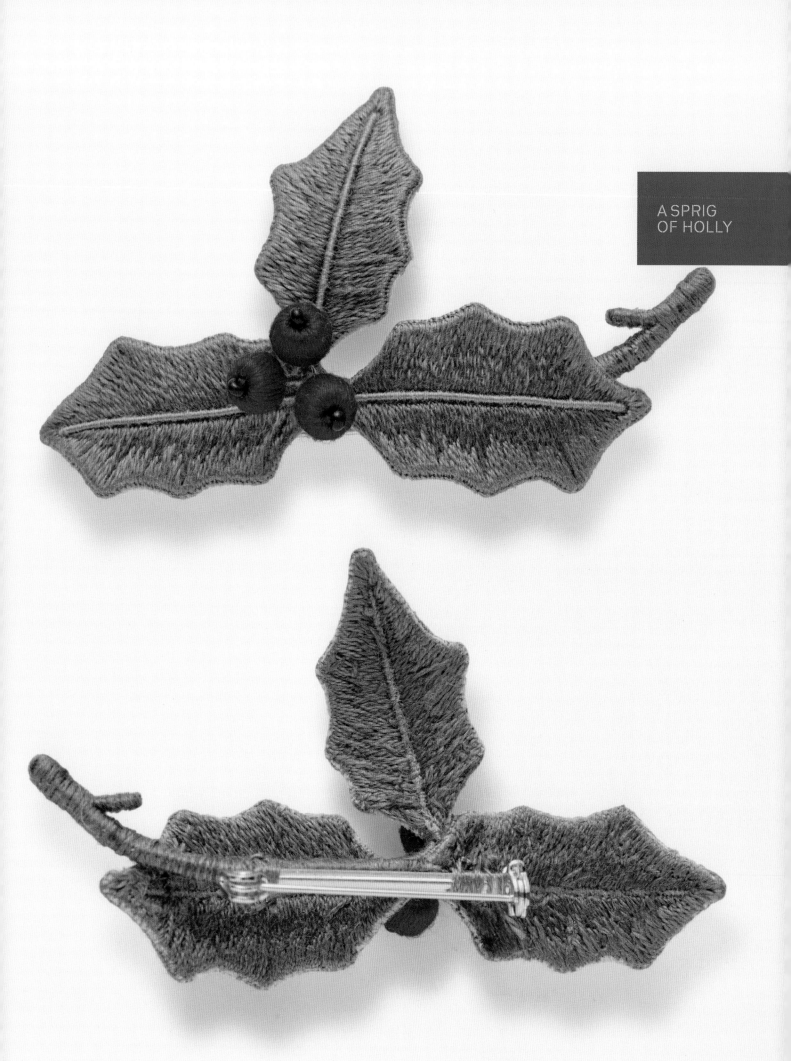

PAT'S BONBON BY HAZEL BLOMKAMP

OVERVIEW

Designer: Hazel Blomkamp	Project: Three-dimensional bonbon	Technique: Bead embroidery
Country of Origin: South Africa	Fabric: Cotton or silk dupion	Threads: Beading threads and beads
Dimensions: 5.5cm x 31cm wide (2⅛" x 12¼")		Design Transfer Required: YES ☐ NO ☒

DESCRIPTION

A fun, festive bonbon that unzips around the centre to reveal
a hiding place for a special gift.

DESIGN NOTES

The bonbon is made over two sections of plastic pipe that
allow it to be opened. The beaded poinsettia and daisy
flowers are made and attached to the fabric before
covering the framework, which is lined with matching
cotton or silk.

TECHNIQUE NOTES

The term beading covers techniques where
beads are sewn directly onto cloth or are
used to create forms or a fabric by being
stitched to one another. The flowers and
leaves use the latter technique and are
worked in the hand then attached to the
fabric. The remaining elements are stitched
directly onto the fabric.

Poinsettia

*The poinsettia (Euphorbia pulcherrima) is indigenous to Mexico and Central
America and its vivid display of bright red bracts against dark green leaves
makes it a Christmas decorating favourite. It grows as a shrub or small tree
and requires periods of darkness to develop the bract colour through a
process known as photoperiodism. The plant's association with Christmas is
thought to have begun in Mexico in the 16th century and it is now cultivated
extensively and is economically the most important potted plant, generating
millions of dollars in sales in the weeks before Christmas. Poinsettias can be
grown in the garden in mild to warm climates and will survive indoors given
consistent conditions and plenty of light.*

FROM THE
DESIGNER

"I had known Pat for perhaps, 30 years and she had worked for me for 15 of those. Aged in her 80s, she enjoyed working two mornings a week and often bragged to others that she still had a job, even at her advanced age. She was the person who watched my business grow, was as excited as I was with the arrival of every newly published book. Every time I went on an overseas teaching trip, she would draw a map of the country I was going to, mark all the towns and point them out to everyone in the studio while I was away.

Pat was a keen quilter and one day in early 2022, she came in to work with a Christmas cracker, made around plastic plumbing pipes, split in the middle with a zip to open and close the two halves, so that it could be stuffed with goodies. She was excited to show the concept to me and said, "I would love to see what you would do with this". It was still sitting on my desk when, on Easter Saturday morning, about to start my car in the grocery store car park, my phone rang. It was her son, to tell me that she had passed away in her sleep. It was such a shock, so unexpected, she had been here on the Wednesday, waved cheerio and drove out. How was this possible? How had I not known that I would never see her again, that I had just waved and not given her a hug, thanked her for everything she had done for me over the years? But it had happened, and I came to the realisation that I was grateful for how it happened. She was active, with her mental faculties intact, right up to what was a gentle end. She deserved that.

Within about a fortnight, I received an email, asking me to consider working up a project for this Christmas book and there was no doubt in my mind that I needed to do a Christmas cracker for Pat, a tribute to her. I pulled her cracker apart and set about reverse engineering it, with no doubt in my mind that it needed beadwork flowers to give it a rich embellishment. Poinsettias are known as Christmas flowers, they were the obvious choice. I worked away on the cracker for a few weeks and suddenly I was getting to the final few stitches, the beaded fringe on the outer edges. Overwhelmingly, I kept wanting to show Pat, ask her what she thought. Then I would realise I can't even send her a picture, no *What's App* where she is. I hope that she would have been impressed with it, that she would have thought it a fitting tribute to a good and much-missed friend."

PAT'S
BONBON

COLOUR PALETTE

PAT'S
BONBON

REQUIREMENTS

Fabric

45cm x 56cm wide
(17¾" x 22") piece of dark
green/black fine
houndstooth cotton or dark
green silk dupion

Supplies

25cm (10") embroidery hoop

20cm x 30cm wide (8" x 12")
piece of dark green wool felt

15cm (6") dark green zip

1m x 25mm wide (40" x 1")
red satin ribbon

Dark green sewing thread

Contrasting sewing thread

Fine beading thread: golden
yellow, red, dark green
and white

7cm x 50mm diameter
(2¾" x 2") pieces of white
PVC plumbing pipe (2)

Seam ripper

Double-sided tape

Ruler

Chalk or ceramic fabric
pencil

Needle

No. 12 bead embroidery

Beads

*Czech 3mm fire-polished
faceted beads*
A = crystal AB (30)

*Miyuki Delica size 11 seed
beads*
B = 602 silver-lined red – 8g

Miyuki size 15 seed beads
C = 17F matte silver-lined
blue green – 2g
D = 457L metallic bronze
light – 2g
E = 551 gilt-lined white opal
– 3g
F = 1422 silver-lined emerald
– 6g
G = 1639 semi-matte silver-
lined red orange – 4g
H = 2425 silver-lined teal
– 3g
I = 4231 duracoat silver-lined
golden flax – 2g

Miyuki 3.4mm drop beads
J = 35 sparkling metallic
gold-lined crystal (20)

PREPARATION
FOR EMBROIDERY

this design uses

Beaded picot chain stitch, p204

Beaded picot edging, p205

Beading, p214

before you begin

We recommend that you read the complete article

All beading is worked with ONE strand of thread

Preparing the fabric

Cut an 11cm (4⅜") strip from the fabric to leave a 45cm (17¾") square. Set the strip aside for construction. Cut the square in half so that you have two rectangles each measuring 45cm x 22.5cm wide (17¾" x 8⅞"). Neaten the raw edges of each piece with a machine zigzag or overlock stitch to prevent fraying.

With right sides together and matching edges, pin and stitch the pieces together along one long edge using a 2cm (¾") seam allowance.

Press the seam open. Lay the fabric with the wrong side facing up. With the wrong side of the zip uppermost, centre it over the seam. Pin and tack in place. Beginning and ending at the upper and lower edges of the fabric, stitch the zip in place 1cm (⅜") from the centre of the zip at each side. Using the fabric pencil and ruler and referring to the diagram, mark a rectangle according to the following measurements. The upper horizontal line is 1cm (⅜") above the end of the zip closure. The lower horizontal line is 17cm (6¹¹⁄₁₆") below the upper line. Each vertical line is 7.5cm (2¹⁵⁄₁₆") from the centre seam line and centre of the zip. The beaded elements will be attached within this marked area.

Using the contrasting sewing thread, tack along the marked lines (diag 1).

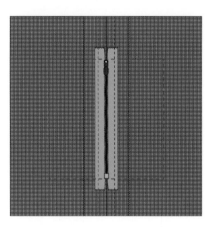

Turn the work to the right side. Using the seam ripper and working carefully, remove the centre seam stitching from between the tacked lines, over the zip. Using the dark green sewing thread, reinforce the seam above and below the opening with hand stitching.

Complete the three-dimensional beading elements.

With the right side facing up, place the fabric in the hoop with the marked rectangle centred, and tension until drum tight, taking care not to distort the tacked lines.

DIAG 3

BEADING

Refer to the close-up photograph for colour placement.

The flowers and leaves are worked in the hand. They are attached and all remaining beading is worked in the hoop.

Order of work

GENERAL BEADING INSTRUCTIONS

For the best results with the structure of the three-dimensional beading, ensure the thread tension remains very tight.

For each element, add beads in numerical order following the diagrams. Set the completed flowers and leaves aside, ready for assembly.

Stopper bead

Before beginning a flower or leaf, thread on a contrasting colour bead and take the thread through it a second time (diag 2).

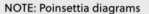

DIAG 2

Position the bead as indicated in the instructions. This acts as a stopper, preventing the initial flower or leaf beads from sliding off the thread tail. Unless otherwise specified, remove when the element is complete.

NOTE: Poinsettia diagrams

Black line = thread path followed as beads are added.

Blue line = when a petal is complete, the path is followed to exit at the petal base..

Green line = beads are already in place and the path is followed to move to the next position for adding beads. Alternatively, the path is followed to attach a new petal to a previous petal or the last petal to the first petal.

POINSETTIAS

Make one each of the 16-bead, 14-bead and 12-bead poinsettias using **B** for the petals with one **G** bead at the tip of each. Each flower has ten petals and is made in a similar manner, changing the number of beads in the petals to create the different sizes.

16-BEAD POINSETTIA

Using a 1.5m (1yd 23") length of red beading thread, position a stopper bead 15cm (6") from one end.

Petal 1

Thread on the first sixteen beads and continue to add beads as shown, noting that bead 32 is a **G** bead (diag 3).

Petal 2

To begin the second petal, attach the first two beads to petal 1 following the green thread path in the diagram. Pick up beads 3–16 and continue to add beads as shown, noting that bead 32 is a **G** bead (diag 4).

Petal 2

Petal 1

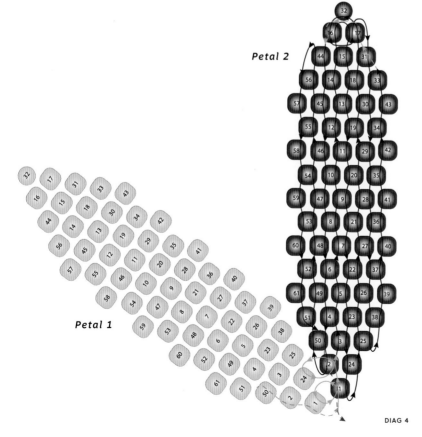

DIAG 4

Petal 3

Add the third petal in the same manner as petal 2 in diagram 4, until you have picked up bead 61 and gone down through bead 51. At this point, fold petal 2 back and attach petal 3 to petal 1 through the lower three beads on the petal edges as shown, ending at the flower centre (diag 5).

Petal 4

Make in the same manner as petal 2.

Petal 5

Make in the same manner as petal 3, folding petal 4 back and attaching petal 5 to petal 3.

Petal 6

Make in the same manner as petal 2.

Petal 7

Make in the same manner as petal 3, folding petal 6 back and attaching petal 7 to petal 5.

Petal 8

Make in the same manner as petal 2.

Petal 9

Make in the same manner as petal 3, folding petal 8 back and attaching petal 9 to petal 7.

Petal 10

Make in the same manner as petal 2. When the petal is complete, follow the blue and green thread paths to attach it to petal 1 (diag 6).

Finishing

Following diagram 5, attach petal 1 to petal 9.

The flower has been constructed from the wrong side. Turn it over so that the right side is facing up and the thread tails at the base are now at the back of the work.

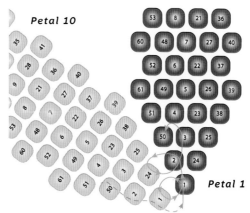

DIAG 6

Set the flower aside, ready for assembly. Do not end off the thread tails.

12-BEAD POINSETTIA

Make one 12-bead poinsettia in a similar manner to the 16-bead poinsettia, picking up twelve beads to begin petal 1 and following the diagram for making each petal, noting that bead 24 is a **G** bead. After adding bead 28, go down through beads 19 and 18. Turn the petal over and continue, beginning by going up through bead 2 and picking up bead 29. Continue to follow the diagram to complete the petal. When complete, turn the petal back over (diag 7).

Continue to make petals in the same manner, referring to diagrams 4, 5 and 6 for attaching them to create a flower with ten petals.

10-BEAD POINSETTIA

Make one 10-bead poinsettia in a similar manner to the 16-bead poinsettia, picking up ten beads to begin petal 1 and following the diagram for making each petal,

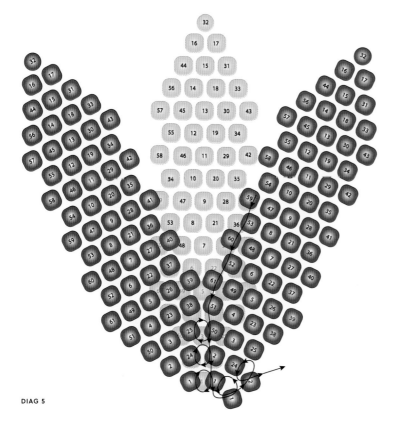

DIAG 5

DIAG 7

noting that bead 20 is a **G** bead. After adding bead 23, go down through beads 16 and 15. Turn the petal over and continue, beginning by going up through bead 2 and picking up bead 24. Continue to follow the diagram to complete the petal. When complete, turn the petal back over (diag 8).

Continue to make petals in the same manner, referring to diagrams 4, 5 and 6 for attaching them to create a flower with ten petals.

DIAG 8

WHITE FLOWERS

Make five flowers in the same manner using **E**.

> **NOTE: White flower diagrams**
> *Pink line* = The path followed to attach a new petal to a previous petal, or the last petal to the first petal

Using a 1.5m (1yd 23") length of white beading thread, position a stopper bead 15cm (6") from one end. Thread on the first six beads and continue to add beads as shown to make the first petal (diag 9).

Add the second petal following the diagram (diag 10).

Add three more petals in the same manner as the second petal. Join the fifth petal to the first through the lower two beads on the adjacent petal edges, returning to the centre as shown (diag 11).

The flower has been constructed from the wrong side. Turn it over so that the right side is facing up and the thread tails at the base are now at the back of the work. Set the flower aside, ready for assembly. Do not end off the thread tails.

LEAVES

Each leaf is made in a similar manner, using **C**, **F** and **H**, changing the number of beads to create the different sizes.

> **HINT:**
> *The original bonbon has seventeen leaves. This can vary. You can make the leaves after you have attached the flowers, deciding what you need as you go along.* HAZEL

Use a 50cm (20") length of dark green beading thread for each leaf and begin by positioning a stopper bead halfway along the thread.

> **NOTE: Leaf diagrams**
> *Pink line* = Change to the second thread tail.

16-BEAD LEAVES

Make one leaf each using **C**, **F** and **H**.

Thread on the first sixteen beads and continue adding beads as shown. After adding bead 43, follow the path to emerge from bead 1 (diag 12).

Removing the stopper bead, change to the second thread tail and turn the leaf over. Follow the thread path through bead 2 to continue adding beads and complete the leaf (diag 13).

Pulling firmly to curl the edges slightly, tie the thread

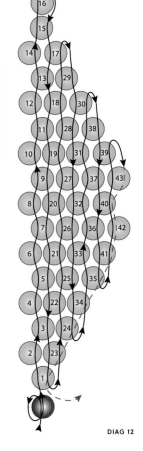

DIAG 12

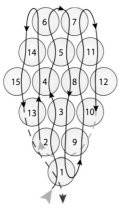

DIAG 9

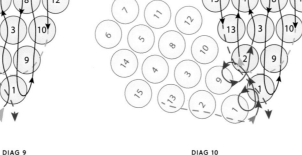

DIAG 10

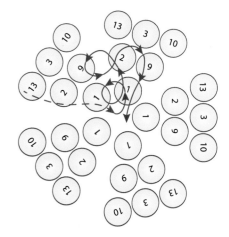

DIAG 11

tails together with a double knot. Do not end off the threads. Set aside for assembly.

14-BEAD LEAVES

Make two using **C**, four using **F** and two using **H** in a similar manner to the 16-bead leaves.

Thread on the first fourteen beads and continue adding beads, removing the stopper bead before changing to the second thread tail where indicated to complete the leaf (diag 14).

Tie off the thread tails in the same manner as the 16-bead leaves.

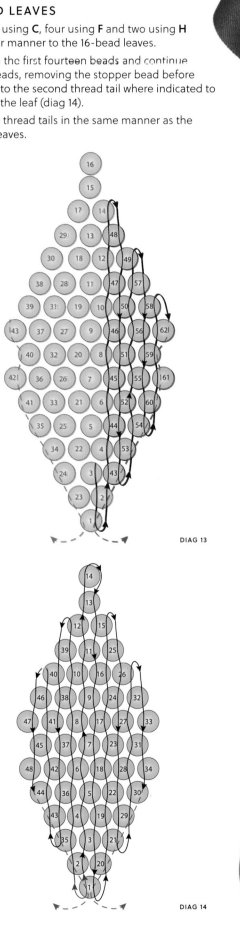

DIAG 13

DIAG 14

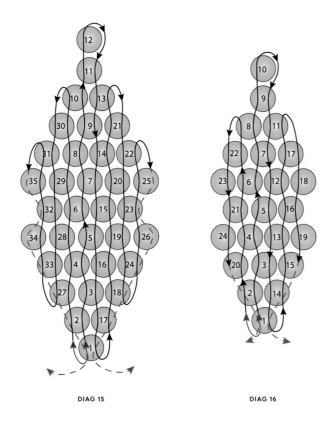

DIAG 15

DIAG 16

12-BEAD LEAF

Make one using **F** in a similar manner to the 16-bead leaves, following the diagram and beginning by threading on twelve beads (diag 15).

Tie off the thread tails in the same manner as before.

10-BEAD LEAVES

Make three using **C** and two using **H** in a similar manner to the 16-bead leaves, following the diagram and beginning by threading on ten beads (diag 16).

Tie off the thread tails in the same manner as before.

ASSEMBLY

When stitching the flowers and leaves to the fabric, do not finish off the threads. Bring the thread tails to the surface away from the working area and leave. Check the arrangement of flowers and leaves, make any desired adjustments, then finish the threads.

Refer to the placement diagram and close-up photograph when positioning each element (diag 17).

Check to ensure the zip can be opened and closed past any overlapping leaf or petal tips.

POINSETTIAS

Position the large flower to the left of the zip and the two smaller flowers to the right of the zip. Secure each flower in the following manner.

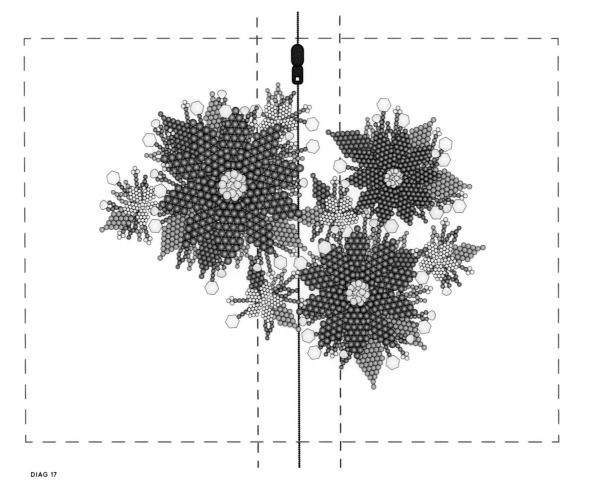

DIAG 17

simple leaves

buds & twigs

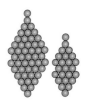

10, 12, 14 and 16 bead leaves

1. Thread one of the two thread tails into the needle. Take the thread through the fabric at the centre of the flower at the desired position.

2. Emerge within the centre beside the join of two petals. Couch over the thread between the two petals and repeat around the circle.

3. Emerge below the third bead from the centre in the middle of one of the petals in the lower layer. Take the needle through the bead and back through the fabric. Repeat to secure each of the lower layer of petals through one bead (diag 18).

Only secure and end off the thread when you are pleased with the overall arrangement. Bring the thread tail to the surface away from the working area. Take the remaining thread tail through the fabric and leave in the same manner.

Flower centre

When the placement has been finalised, use the golden yellow beading thread and **I** to work the large flower centre in the following manner.

1. Emerge between two beads between the third and fourth row of beads in an upper layer petal.

2. Thread on an **I** bead and couch over the thread between two beads of the third row, taking the needle to the back between the second and third rows. Repeat around the flower, adding beads over the lower layer where necessary, to create a circle of yellow beads.

3. Working inwards, attach beads between the petal beads in the same manner, row by row.

4. Attach beads to fill the centre and stitch additional beads over the top of the previous beads to create a domed shape (diag 19).

Work the centres for the smaller flowers in a similar manner, beginning closer to the base of the petals.

WHITE FLOWERS

Use the thread tails to secure three flowers around the large poinsettia and two flowers between the small poinsettias. When placement has been finalised, use the golden yellow beading thread to stitch an **I** bead at the centre of each flower.

LEAVES

Attach each leaf in the following manner.

1. Using one of the thread tails, take the needle through the fabric so that the base of the leaf will be tucked beneath a flower petal.

2. Emerge beneath the third bead from the base along the leaf centre. Take the needle through the bead and back through the fabric.

3. Emerge between two beads at the leaf edge, two or three beads up from the base. Couch over the thread between the beads. Repeat on the opposite side of the leaf (diag 20).

When you are pleased with the arrangement of flowers and leaves, secure and end off all thread tails.

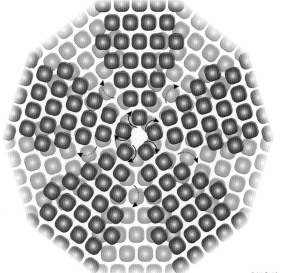

DIAG 18

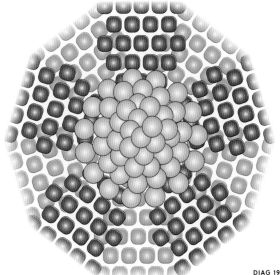

DIAG 19

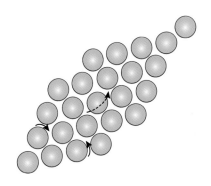

DIAG 20

SMALL ELEMENTS

Using the dark green beading thread, surround the flowers and leaves with simple leaves, twigs and buds as desired, emerging from beneath the petals and leaves (diag 21).

Refer to the diagrams for making the different elements, using the following beads and varying the number in the stems as desired.

SIMPLE LEAVES: eleven **F** or **H**

CRYSTAL BUDS: three-nine **F**, one **A**, one **F**

DROP BEAD BUDS: three-nine **D**, one **J**, two **D**

TWIGS: three-nine **D**, three **I**

simple leaves

crystal buds

drop bead buds

twigs

DIAG 21

CONSTRUCTION

All seam allowances are 1cm (⅜"). The shaded areas on the following diagrams indicate the right side of the fabric.

Covering the cylinders with felt

From the felt cut two rectangles, each 9cm x 16.5cm wide (3½" x 6½"). On the remaining felt, use one of the cylinder lengths to trace two circles using the fabric marker and cut out.

Wrap one piece of cylinder with one rectangle of felt, aligning one long edge with one end, so that the short ends butt up against each other. If the edges overlap, trim so that they just meet. Using the dark green sewing thread, hand stitch the short ends of the felt together.

Position one circle of felt over the end of the covered cylinder that has the felt aligned with the edge and hand stitch in place using the same thread (diag 1).

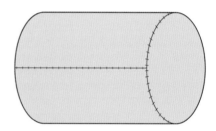

At the opposite end, apply double-sided adhesive tape to the inside of the cylinder, just below the edge. Trim the overlapping felt so that there is a 1cm (⅜") seam allowance. Fold the seam allowance to the inside of the pipe and press firmly to secure to the adhesive tape (diag 2).

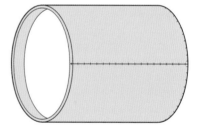

Repeat to cover the remaining cylinder.

Lining the cylinders

From the 11cm (4⅜") wide strip of fabric cut two rectangles, each measuring 15.5cm x 9cm wide (6⅛" x 3½"). With right sides facing, fold one rectangle in half, aligning the short edges. Pin and stitch the short edges together and press the seam open. Pin and stitch one long edge together. With the right side still facing inwards, fold the remaining seam allowance to the wrong side and finger press (diag 3).

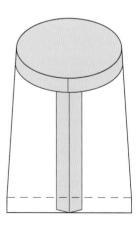

Slide the lining down inside one felt-covered cylinder until the folded edge of the fabric is aligned with the folded edge of the felt. Hand stitch the lining to the felt around the folded edges using the dark green sewing thread (diag 4).

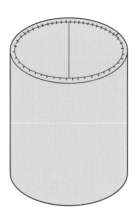

Repeat to line the remaining felt-covered cylinder.

Preparing the bead-embroidered fabric

Remove the fabric from the hoop and press, using a pressing cloth and avoiding the beading. With the right side facing outwards and the zip aligned with the circumference, wrap the beaded fabric around the prepared cylinders to check the fit. The lines of tacking above and below zip should meet. Adjust the lines of tacking if necessary. Measure out 1cm (⅜") from each horizontal line of tacking and trim away the excess fabric.

Measure out 12cm (4¾") from each vertical tacked line and rule a line using the fabric marker. Trim away the excess fabric and neaten the raw edge with a machine zigzag or overlock stitch (diag 5).

Covering the cylinder with the beaded fabric

With right sides facing, carefully align the horizontal tacked lines above and below the zip opening. Pin and stitch along the tacked lines. Neaten the seam allowance.

Turn the fabric to the right side. Working from each end, insert the prepared cylinders into the fabric tube until the open ends meet, aligned with the centre of the zip.

At each end of the fabric tube, fold in 5mm (³⁄₁₆"). Fold in a further 1cm (⅜") and press to create a hem. Hand stitch the first fold in place to secure using the dark green sewing thread. At one end of the tube, measure 2.5cm (1") from the end of the cylinder, and leaving a tail at each end, work a line running stitch using the same thread. Pull up the thread tails, gathering the fabric, and tie off firmly (diag 6).

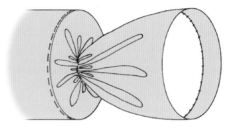

Repeat at the remaining end of the tube.

Beading

Using the dark green beading thread, **B** and **F**, and referring to the step-by-step instructions on page 204, embroider beaded picot chain stitch at each end of the cylinder, using the line of tacking at each end as a guide. Use a scooping motion with the needle to move to the required positions, as the cylinder prevents stab stitching. The beaded line should be just in from the edge at each end.

Using the same beading thread and **F** and **G**, embroider beaded picot edging along the fold at each end of the bonbon, following the step-by-step instructions on page 205.

Finishing

Cut the length of red satin ribbon in half. Tie one half in a neat bow around the gathering at each side of the bonbon and trim the tails at an angle.

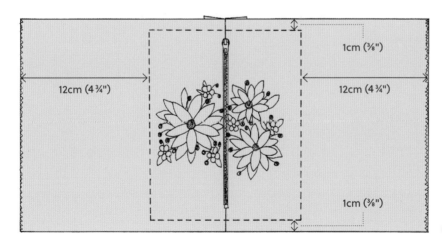

12cm (4¾")   1cm (⅜")

12cm (4¾")   1cm (⅜")

DIAG 5

A SUMMER CHRISTMAS
BY
ANA MALLAH

OVERVIEW

Designer:	Project:	Technique:
Ana Mallah	Floral wreath	Stumpwork
Country of Origin:	**Fabric:**	**Threads:**
Australia	Linen	Stranded cotton

Dimensions:	
14cm x 16cm wide (5½" x 6¼")	**Design Transfer Required:** YES ☒ NO ☐

DESCRIPTION

A delicate, embroidered garland with papery hydrangea flowers and plump snowberries arranged on a circle of twigs.

DESIGN NOTES

A gentle celebration of the seasonal variation at Christmas between the Northern and Southern Hemispheres, the winter fruiting snow berries are combined with summer-flowering hydrangea, flora that appears at the same time in December in different parts of the world.

TECHNIQUE NOTES

Stumpwork techniques are combined with surface stitching to add dimension and enable the elements to be manipulated in various ways. Leaves and hydrangea sepals have wired margins that are concealed by the embroidery and can be easily shaped as desired. Berries are worked over felt balls that provide a surface that can be stitched into to create shading and small details. Glass seed beads are used to finish the centres of the hydrangea flowers and berries.

Christmas in Australia

Occurring in summer, an Australian Christmas draws partly from the traditions of the Northern Hemisphere while embracing the unique environment and conditions of a large, sunny continent. While holly, reindeer, snow-covered landscapes, fir trees and rosy-cheeked carol singers, rugged up against the cold, still make the occasional appearance on cards and decorations, many Australians have embraced their indigenous flora and fauna and the delights of warm December weather to create a unique celebration. A seafood feast has replaced the Christmas turkey and food is more likely to be served cold than hot. Steaming Christmas pudding has made way for an ice cream version or a lavish pavlova, decorated with lashings of cream and luscious summer fruits such as mango, passionfruit and raspberries. Although things have changed and habits have evolved, the spirit of Christmas remains the same here as in other parts of the world.

FROM THE DESIGNER

"I will usually draw out ideas and maybe put colour to them. Sometimes the finished embroidery is very different from what I originally scribbled on paper. With this design, I had a clear picture in my head and was quite certain of the colours, so it more or less followed my basic, original sketch.

Once I knew the direction I was headed with the design, it was time to think about threads and colours. This is one of the most exciting aspects of preparing for a new design. Often, new colours will present themselves and beg to be included into the mix and I simply cannot turn them down! The colours and subject matter of this design came to me whilst having a conversation with a friend. Last summer she had come across a bunch of hydrangea and snowberries. She was describing them in such detail that I started to form an idea as she was talking. Several months later, I was asked if I might contribute something to a Christmas publication and the idea my friend had inspired me with instantly came to mind. For me, these colours remind me of our Christmas here in Australia. Christmas and the beach are intertwined and the cool blues and greens of a hydrangea remind me of this. The snowberries remind me of a more traditional, Northern Hemisphere Christmas. Putting these two elements together I thought, perfectly suited our Christmas here in Melbourne. We are known for four seasons in one day, so we are equally as likely to have Christmas by the beach or by a fireplace. One can never quite tell what we'll get!"

A SUMMER CHRISTMAS

COLOUR PALETTE

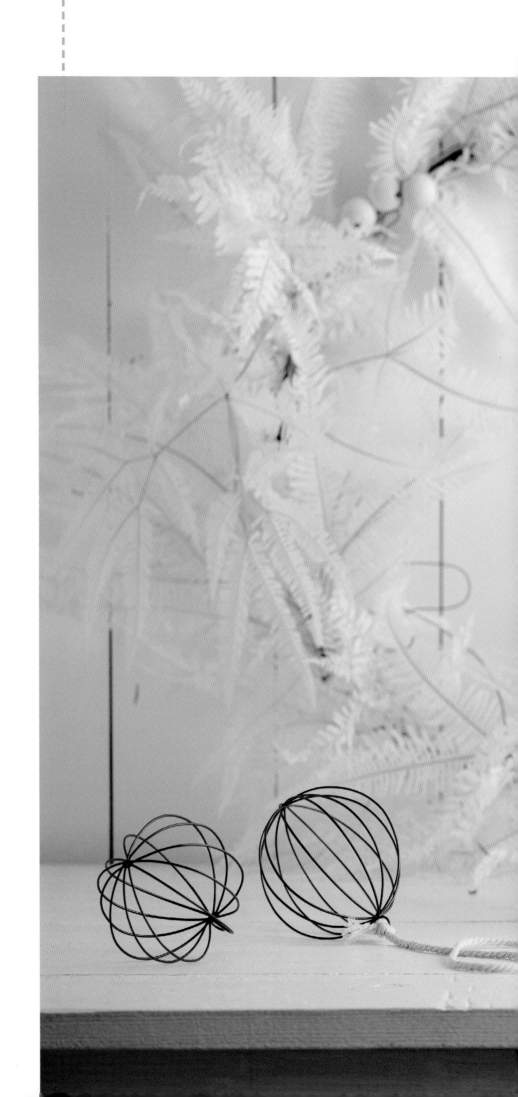

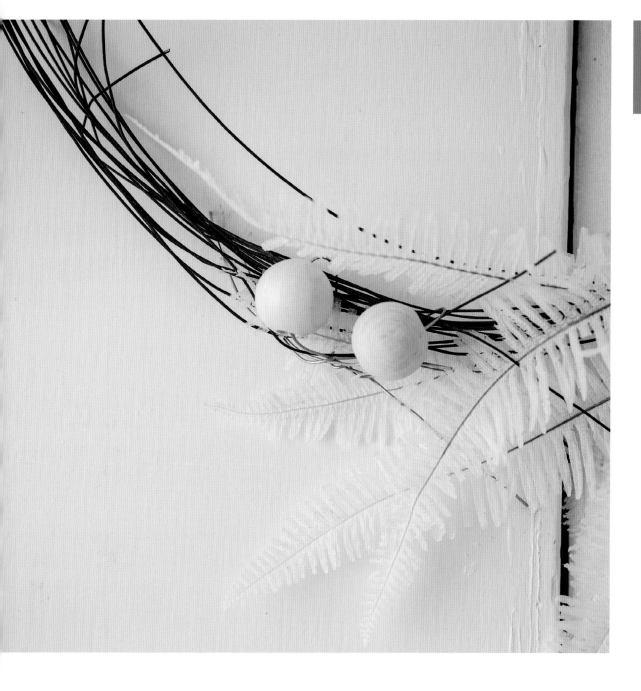

Hydrangea + Snowberries

Ana Mallah

REQUIREMENTS

Fabric

45cm (18") square of ivory linen

45cm x 65cm wide (18" x 26") piece of quilter's muslin

Supplies

12.5cm (5") embroidery hoop

25cm (10") embroidery hoop

36cm (14") lengths of 33 gauge white paper-covered wire (12)

1cm (⅜") diameter natural wool felt balls (10)

Dressmaker's awl

Fine sharp embroidery scissors

Scissors to cut wire

Acid-free glue stick

Tracing paper

Fine black pen

Fine heat-soluble fabric marker

Needles

No. 6 crewel

No. 9 crewel

No. 10 sharp

Threads & Beads

Classic Colorworks
stranded cotton
A = 152 olive branch

DMC *stranded cotton*
B = 632 vy dk mocha
C = 838 dk beige-brown
D = 839 med beige-brown
E = 840 beige-brown
F = 841 lt beige-brown
G = 842 vy lt beige-brown
H = 3346 hunter green
I = 3347 med yellow-green
J = 3348 lt yellow-green
K = 3362 dk pine green
L = 3790 ultra dk beige-grey
M = 3865 winter white
N = blanc

***The Gentle Art Simply
Shaker*** *stranded cotton*
O = 0920 tropical ocean
P = 7089 tradewind

Threadworx *overdyed
stranded cotton*
Q = 1060 green tea latte
R = 11351 cotton candy

Miyuki *size 11 seed beads*
S = 135F frosted transparent brown (10)
T = 4697 frosted opaque glaze rainbow olive (8)

Toho *size 11 seed bead*
U = Y310 hybrid sour apple Picasso (1)

this design uses

Blanket stitch, p214

Long and short blanket stitch, p214

Long and short stitch, p215

Split stitch, p215

Straight stitch, p215

Wrapping

before you begin

See the liftout pattern for the embroidery design and templates

We recommend that you read the complete article

All embroidery is worked with ONE strand of thread unless specified

PREPARATION FOR EMBROIDERY

Preparing the fabrics

From the quilter's muslin cut one 45cm (18") square to back the embroidery and two, 20cm (8") squares for the detached elements. Neaten the edges of the linen and quilter's muslin squares using a machine zigzag or overlock stitch to prevent fraying.

Transferring the design

MAIN DESIGN

Using the black pen, transfer the design and placement marks onto tracing paper. Tape the tracing to a lightbox or window. Centre the linen over the design, aligning the placement marks with the straight grain and transfer the design using the fine, heat-soluble fabric marker. With the design side uppermost and matching edges, position the linen over the quilter's muslin and place both fabrics in the 25cm (10") hoop, tensioning both fabrics until the surface is drum tight.

DETACHED ELEMENTS

Using the black pen, transfer the leaf and hydrangea sepal outlines onto tracing paper.

Centre the inner ring of the 12.5cm (5") hoop onto one square of quilter's muslin. Using the heat-soluble marker, trace around the inner edge of the ring to mark a circle. Working within the marked circle, transfer the shaping for the leaves and ten of the sepals using the heat-soluble fabric marker and varying the sepal sizes. Repeat with the second piece of quilter's muslin, transferring the remaining twenty-one sepals within the marked circle.

Place the fabric with the leaves and sepals in the 12.5cm (5") hoop and tension until drum tight, taking care not to distort the shapes. Once the leaf and sepal embroidery is complete place the second piece of fabric in the 12.5cm (5") hoop and complete the remaining elements.

EMBROIDERY

Refer to the close-up photograph for colour and stitch placement.

Use the no. 6 crewel needle for 2-3 strands of thread, the no. 9 crewel for one strand of thread and the no. 10 sharp needle for attaching the beads.

All embroidery is worked in a hoop.

Order of work

WREATH

Using **C**, outline the inner edge of one twig with split stitch. Mark in the breaks and scars with straight stitch using the same thread. Work a second line of split stitch inside the first using **E** then lines using **L**, **F** and **G**. Fill any remaining space with lines of split stitch, shading back through **F** and **L**. Outline the outer edge of the twig

with split stitch using **D**. Work the remaining twigs in the same manner, using the photograph as a guide to colour placement. Outline the end of each twig with split stitch using **C** or **D** and fill with straight stitch using **F**.

SNOWBERRIES

Berry

On one felt ball, mark a 5mm (³⁄₁₆") circle on one end for the top of the berry and a 1mm (¹⁄₃₂") circle at the opposite end for the base using the fine, heat-soluble fabric marker. Using two strands of **M** and one of **N** together in the needle, work straight stitches around the ball to cover the surface, leaving the marked areas free of stitching (fig 1).

Take the needle through the ball and trim the thread close to the surface.

Using two strands of **R** and keeping the small, unstitched area clear, work long and short stitch around the base of the berry, bringing the long stitches one third of the way down the berry and the short stitches approximately half that length.

At the top of the berry, bring the same thread to the surface in the large, unstitched area, 2mm (¹⁄₁₆") from the edge of the white stitching. Work long and short blanket stitch around the top, extending the longest stitches approximately halfway down the berry, with the beaded edge forming a circle around the top (fig 2).

Using the dressmaker's awl, form an opening at the base of the berry, inserting the awl through the unstitched area and making the opening as deep as you can. Thread two strands of **L** into the needle and knot the end of the thread. Take the needle up through the base of the berry, emerge through the top then take the needle back down through the berry and emerge through the base. Pull the thread firmly to ensure that it is secured. Cut a 10cm (4") length of wire and fold in half. Take the thread under the wire fold and back up through the base and out through the top of the berry

1mm (¹⁄₃₂") inside the beaded edge of the pink stitches. Pull the thread firmly to draw the wire fold into the opening as far as possible (fig 3).

Work blanket stitch into the beaded edge of the pink stitches using the two strands of **L** (fig 4).

Take the needle down through the berry and emerge through the base then back up through the berry, taking care to ensure that the thread is between the two wire tails, emerging just to one side of the centre top. Using the same thread, attach an **S** bead at the centre of the berry top (fig 5).

Prepare the remaining nine berries in the same manner.

Stem

Cut two, 30cm (12") strands of **B**. Fold in half and bring the ends together. Using the glue stick and beginning at the base of the berry, coat three quarters of the wire length with a very thin layer of glue. Place the looped end of the thread behind the stem wires (fig 6).

Pass the thread tails through the loop and pull firmly to secure. Wrap the wire firmly for three-quarters of the length, taking care to ensure that it is completely covered. Secure the thread with a half hitch and leave to dry. Trim away the thread tails. Make the stems on the remaining berries in the same manner.

Leaves

Leaving a 3cm (1⅛") tail at each end, couch a length of wire around one leaf shape using **K**. Using the same thread and beginning at the base of the leaf on the right-hand side, work close blanket stitch over the wire for approximately 1cm (⅜") then continue working close long and short blanket stitch around the outer edge, angling the stitches towards the base of the leaf (fig 7).

Continue working in this manner around the outer edge of the leaf until reaching the corresponding point on the second side then cover the remaining wire to the leaf base with close blanket stitch (fig 8).

FIG 1

FIG 2

FIG 3

FIG 4

FIG 5

FIG 6

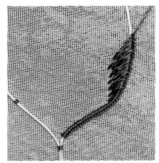
FIG 7

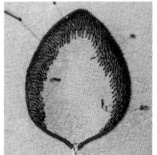
FIG 8

Fill the leaf with rows of long and short stitch, shading from **H** to **I**. Work the centre and side veins with split stitch using **J**.

HYDRANGEA

There are thirty-one sepals required with some flowers having three sepals while others have four.

Work the following sepals:

10 sepals using **A**

7 sepals using **O**

6 sepals using **P**

8 sepals using **Q**

All sepals are worked in the following manner.

Cut a 7cm (2¾") length of wire. Fold the wire in half to form a point then open out. Beginning with the fold at the tip of the sepal, couch the wire in place, working a stitch over both wires at the base. Beginning on the right-hand side of the base, work twelve close blanket stitches over the wire. Begin working close long and short blanket stitch around the outer two-thirds of the sepal, angling the stitches towards the base, until reaching the corresponding point on the second side (fig 9).

FIG 9

Cover the remaining wire to the sepal base with close blanket stitch then fill the unstitched area on the sepal with long and short stitch. Using **L**, work 3–4 long straight stitches into the base of the sepal.

ASSEMBLING THE SNOWBERRY SPRAY

Cut out the leaves using the fine, sharp embroidery scissors following the step-by-step instructions on page 207.

Cut two, 80cm (31½") strands of **B**. Fold in half and bring the ends together. Using the glue stick and beginning 1cm (⅜") down from the base of one berry, coat the wire length with a very thin layer of glue. Place the looped end of the thread behind the stem wires and pass the thread tails through the loop and pull firmly to secure. Wrap the thread firmly around the wire for 3mm (⅛"). Leaving a 6mm (¼") stem on a second berry, place the stems together and wrap twice. Leaving a 3mm (⅛") stem on a third berry, place the stems together and wrap all the wires for 1cm (⅜"), adding glue to the wires where necessary. Coat the wires on one small leaf stem with a thin layer of glue, add to the berry stems and wrap all the wires for 2cm (¾").

> **NOTE:** If running out of wrapping thread, glue the thread ends to the wires and join in a new wrapping thread in the same manner as before.

Leaving an 8mm (⁵⁄₁₆") stem, add in a fourth berry and wrap for 4mm (⁵⁄₃₂") then, leaving a 3mm (⅛") stem, add in a fifth berry and wrap all the wires for 3mm (⅛"). Coat the wires on the large leaf stem with a thin layer of glue, add to the berry stems and wrap all the wires for 1.5cm (⅝"). Leaving a 5mm (³⁄₁₆") stem, add in a sixth berry and wrap for 4mm (⁵⁄₃₂"), then, leaving a 2mm (¹⁄₁₆") stem, add in a seventh berry and wrap for 3mm (⅛"). Coat the wires on the remaining small leaf stem with a thin layer of glue, add to the berry stems and wrap all the wires for 2cm (¾"). Leaving a 5mm (³⁄₁₆") stem on an eighth berry and a 3mm (⅛") stem on a ninth berry, add both berries and wrap all the wires for 5mm (³⁄₁₆"). Leaving a 5mm (³⁄₁₆") stem add in the final berry and wrap all the wires for 1.5cm (⅝") (diag 1).

DIAG 1

A 3mm (⅛")

B 4mm (⁵⁄₃₂")

C 5mm (³⁄₁₆")

D 1cm (⅜")

E 1.5cm (⅝")

F 2cm (¾")

G 2 wraps

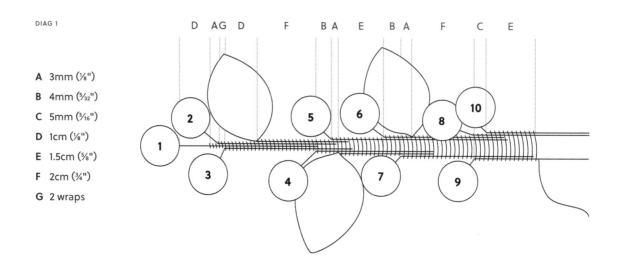

Do not trim away the thread.

Coat the remaining wires with a thin layer of glue and bend the ends of the wire tails back on themselves to form a loop. Continue wrapping to the end of the stem then wrap around the loop, feeding the thread down through the centre, until it is completely covered. Wrap over the loop to flatten and cover it and back up the stem for 5mm (³⁄₁₆"). Secure the thread with a half hitch knot and a small dab of glue. Allow to dry and trim away the excess thread. The finished stem should measure approximately 13cm (5¼").

ASSEMBLING THE HYDRANGEA FLOWERS

Remove the fabric from the hoop and carefully cut out each sepal using the fine, sharp embroidery scissors and following the step-by-step instructions on page 207. Thread the **U** bead onto a 20cm (8") length of **Q**.

Adjust the bead so that it is sitting at the centre of the thread and thread both ends of the strand into a needle. Coat the wire tails of one **P** sepal with a thin layer of glue. Place the looped end of the thread with the bead behind the sepal wires and pass the thread tails through the loop and pull firmly to secure, taking care to ensure that the bead stays at the base of the sepal. Wrap the wires once. Bend the sepal back (fig 10).

FIG 10

Add in a second **P** sepal and wrap all the wires once then add in a third **P** sepal and wrap all the wires 2–3 times. Continue wrapping the wires for at least 2cm (¾"), adding more glue if necessary. Secure the wrapping thread with a half hitch knot and a small dab of glue. Allow to dry. Assemble the remaining flowers in a similar manner using the **T** beads and the photograph as a guide to sepal numbers.

ASSEMBLING THE WREATH

Hydrangea

Use the dressmaker's awl to carefully pierce a hole in the fabric then insert the wires for one four-sepal hydrangea just to the left of the centre at the base of the wreath. Bend the wire tails back under the wreath and secure through the backing fabric. Using the photograph as a guide, add five more flowers along the lower left-hand side in the same manner. Before attaching the next flower, trim the wire tails to the end of the wrapping. Position the flower and stem on the fabric surface and couch the stem in place using **Q**. The end of the stem should be concealed under the lower flowers. Attach the next flower in the same manner as the first six, inserting the stem through the fabric and bending the wire tails back behind the wreath and securing to the backing fabric. Trim the wire tails of the final flower to the end of the wrapping and couch the stem on the fabric surface using **Q**. The end of the stem should be concealed beneath the sepals of the previous flower.

Snowberries

Carefully bend the snowberry stem to echo the curve of the wreath. Tuck the end of the stem behind the sepals of the centre hydrangea flowers and using two strands of **B**, couch the stem in place at 1cm (³⁄₈") intervals (fig 11).

FIG 11

The top of the upper berry should sit approximately 1.5cm (⅝") below the centre of the upper hydrangea.

FINISHING

Once the embroidery is laced onto firm card shape the sepals and leaves as desired.

FOLK ART BIRD ORNAMENT BY TRISH BURR

OVERVIEW

Designer:	Project:	Technique:
Trish Burr	Hanging ornament	Surface embroidery
Country of Origin:	**Fabric:**	**Threads:**
South Africa	Cotton	Stranded cotton
Dimensions: 10cm (4") in diameter	**Design Transfer Required:** YES ☒ NO ☐	

DESCRIPTION

A circular hanging ornament with a bird and flower motifs worked with an unusual palette of garnet, persimmon and grey-green.

DESIGN NOTES

Borrowing from the clean forms of Scandinavian folk art, the bird is filled with various patterns and surrounded by flowers and tiny snowflakes. The ornament is finished with a beaded edge and a striped ribbon ties in a bow at the base of the hanging loop.

TECHNIQUE NOTES

Padding is used to add surface interest to some areas worked with satin stitch. Subtle, long and short stitch shading offers a gentle contrast to the blocks of solid colour and strong, split stitch outlines accentuate the simple forms and define the design. Brick stitch beaded edging is worked around the ornament using red glass seed beads and this colour is echoed in the stranded cotton hanging loop and ribbon bow.

Scandinavian Folk Art

The origins of Scandinavian folk art date back to the Viking Age and the style is thought to be influenced by traditional Nordic designs and mythologies. Common elements include geometric patterns, motifs from nature such as flowers, leaves, and animals, particularly birds, fish and horses, and symbols from folklore and mythology. Bright, contrasting colours are used and the elements are often highly stylised and utilise simple shapes. Using these designs, rural craftsman created functional and decorative objects such as household furniture, toys, textiles and ceramics for everyday use. The 19th and 20th centuries saw a revival of interest in traditional folk art that introduced new designs and techniques and these remain popular today.

FROM THE DESIGNER

"I know that Christmas is a busy time and therefore wanted to provide a project that could be completed fairly quickly. My thought process was that I would keep the colour scheme simple for two reasons: 1. It would be more cost effective 2. If the reader wanted to stitch up a couple of ornaments as gifts for friends they could easily change the colour scheme for each one, so providing variety. I tend to get bored stitching the same project more than once! I was inspired by the simplicity of Scandinavian designs, so licensed an image from an online stock images company, which I used as the basis of my design. I draw all my designs in *Corel Draw*, as I can amend them to fit into the required space, try out different colours and get an idea of what they look like before I stitch them. Saves a great deal of unpicking or starting again! Beading is not really my thing but it did provide the perfect finish."

FOLK ART
BIRD
ORNAMENT

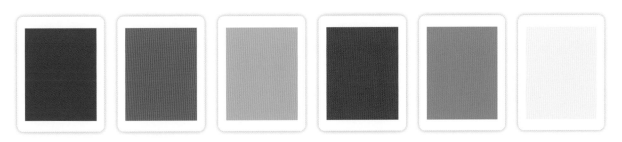

COLOUR PALETTE

FOLK ART
BIRD
ORNAMENT

96/1

REQUIREMENTS

Fabric

20cm (8") square of white cotton

15cm (6") square of coordinating print cotton

Supplies

15cm (6") embroidery hoop

11cm x 22cm wide (4 ⅜" x 8 ⅝") piece of white wool felt

25cm x 9mm wide (10" x ⅜") red and white striped ribbon

12cm x 24cm wide (4 ¾" x 9 ½") piece of white card

White sewing thread

Light-coloured sewing thread

Craft glue

Tracing paper

Fine black pen

Fine heat-soluble fabric marker

Needle

No. 10 sharp

Threads & Beads

DMC no. 30 broder spécial
A = blanc

DMC stranded cotton
B = 321 vy lt garnet
C = 498 med garnet
D = 921 copper
E = 924 vy dk grey-green
F = 926 med grey-green
G = 3768 dk grey-green
H = 3799 vy dk pewter grey
I = 3801 vy dk melon
J = 3853 persimmon
K = 3854 lt persimmon

Mill Hill glass seed beads
L = 03043 oriental red

this design uses

Brick stitch beaded edging, p206

Dot stitch, p208

Long and short stitch, p215

Padded satin stitch, p210

Satin stitch, p215

Satin stitch dot, p212

Split stitch, p215

Trellis couching, p215

before you begin

See the liftout pattern for the embroidery design and circle template

We recommend that you read the complete article

All embroidery is worked with ONE strand of thread

- - - - -
PREPARATION FOR EMBROIDERY

Preparing the fabric

Wash and press the white cotton before transferring the design. Neaten the raw edges with a machine zigzag or overlock stitch to prevent fraying.

Transferring the design

Using the black pen transfer the embroidery design, cutting line and placement marks onto tracing paper. Centre the white cotton over the design, aligning the placement marks with the straight grain. Using a lightbox or window if necessary, trace the design and cutting line onto the cotton with the heat-soluble fabric marker. Using the light-coloured sewing thread, tack along the cutting line. Place the fabric in the hoop and tension until the surface is drum tight, ensuring the grainlines remain straight.

- - - - -
EMBROIDERY

Refer to the close-up photograph for colour and stitch placement.

All embroidery is worked in the hoop.

Order of work

TAIL FEATHERS

Fill the lower teardrop section of each feather with long and short stitch beginning at the outer edge with **I** and shading through **B** to **C** at the base. Outline each teardrop with split stitch using **H**.

Fill the outer section of each feather with padded satin stitch using **A**. Beginning and ending at the base section, complete each tail feather outline with split stitch using **G**. Embroider dot stitch within the remaining area in each feather using **A**, following the curve.

> **NOTE: Padded satin stitch**
>
> Begin by outlining each shape with split stitch or two rows of running stitch, the second row splitting through the first. To create a slightly raised effect, work one layer of padding perpendicular to the satin stitch. To create a plump, domed effect, work more than one layer of padding to create the desired result, ensuring the final padding layer is perpendicular to the satin stitch.

WING

Flower

Fill the triangular sections around the outer edge of the petals with padded satin stitch using **B**. Outline the upper edge of each triangle with split stitch using **H**. Embroider each petal with padded satin stitch using **A** and outline with split stitch using **K**, omitting the upper petal sections along the edge of the bird's back.

Fill the flower centre with padded satin stitch using **K** and outline the upper edge with split stitch using **H**. Embroider four satin stitch dots above the centre using **B** and outline with split stitch using **G**.

Bands

Fill the grey band below the flower with long and short stitch, beginning at the tail end using **F** and shading through **G** to **E** in the narrow section.

Beginning at the upper end, fill the orange band with long and short stitch, shading from **K** through **J** to **D**. Outline the upper edge with split stitch using **H**.

Embroider the area above the orange band with padded satin stitch using **A**, working the final satin stitch layer across the shape. Outline the right-hand edge with split stitch using **H**, extending the line along the right-hand edge of the orange band.

Fill the domed shapes in the right-hand band with padded satin stitch using **I**. Embroider the remainder of the band with satin stitch using **F** and outline the right-hand edge with split stitch using **H**. Work a line of split stitch down the left-hand side using **A**.

> **NOTE: Satin stitch**
> To create a well-defined edge, outline each shape with split stitch before covering with satin stitch.

BREAST, COLLAR AND NECK

Embroider the breast with satin stitch using **B**.

Work the collar with padded satin stitch using **A** and outline the upper edge with split stitch using **H**.

Fill the neck with vertical satin stitch using **F**. Cover the satin stitch with trellis couching, using **A** for the long, straight stitches, spacing them 2mm (1/16") apart. Couch each intersection with a horizontal straight stitch using **B**.

MAIN OUTLINE AND LEGS

Beginning at the upper edge, where the neck meets the head, outline the bird with split stitch using **H**, working to the tip of the body and back along the lower edge to the point where the neck meets the head.

Fill the legs with rows of split stitch using **G**.

HEAD

Omitting the eye area, fill the circular head section with padded satin stitch using **K**, working the satin stitch horizontally over one layer of padding. Outline the outer edge of the satin stitch with split stitch using **G**, omitting the section beside the beak.

Embroider the inner eye circle with padded satin stitch using **H**, working the satin stitches horizontally. Stitch the highlight with two tiny straight stitches using **A** and outline the eye with split stitch using **B**. Work a split stitch outline around the eye using **A** and a second outline in the same manner using **H**.

Stitch the beak with horizontal satin stitch using **E**.

Fill the band on the left-hand side of the head with padded satin stitch using **A**, ensuring the previous head outline remains uncovered. Outline the left-hand edge with split stitch using **G**.

TULIP

Beginning at the upper edge, fill the centre with long and short stitch, shading from **K** to **J**. Outline the upper edge with split stitch using **H**. Fill each petal with padded satin stitch using **A** and outline with split stitch using **H**.

Fill each leaf with padded stain stitch using **G** and outline with split stitch using **H**. Stitch the stem with rows of split stitch using the same thread.

BLOSSOMS

Embroider each blossom centre with padded satin stitch using **K** and outline with split stitch using **H**. Stitch the petals with padded satin stitch, working three petals of each flower using **I** and two petals using **B**.

SNOWFLAKES

Stitch the spokes with straight stitch using **F** and add a two-wrap French knot to each tip using the same thread.

CONSTRUCTION

All seam allowances are 1.5cm (⅝") unless specified. The shaded areas on the following diagrams indicate the right side of the fabric.

Preparing the embroidered fabric

Remove the embroidered cotton from the hoop and press, face down into a soft, padded surface. Cut out along the tacked line.

Cutting out the print cotton

Using the embroidered cotton as a template, cut a circle from the print cotton.

Preparing the card

Using the circle template, cut two pieces each of card and white felt. If desired, use a small piece of sandpaper to smooth the edges of the card. Trim away approximately 1mm (¹⁄₃₂") from around the felt circles. Glue one circle of felt to one side of each card circle (diag 1).

Weight the padded circles with heavy books until dry.

Covering the card

Leaving a tail at each end, work a line of running stitch 7mm (⁵⁄₁₆") in from the cut edge. With the padded side facing the fabric, centre the card over the wrong side of

the embroidered cotton. Pull up the gathering threads firmly and tie off securely. Lace the seam allowance over the card (diag 2).

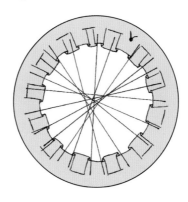

Repeat to cover the remaining card with the print cotton.

Assembling the ornament

Cut a 20cm (8") length of all six strands of **B**. Fold in half and knot the tails together near the tips. Stitch the knotted end of the loop to the seam allowance of the print cotton, leaving a loop for hanging.

Matching edges and with wrong sides together, position the embroidered card over the print cotton card, ensuring the embroidery is oriented correctly. Using the white sewing thread, ladder stitch the two circles together around the outer edge.

Finishing

Using **B** and **L**, and referring to the step-by-step instructions on page 206, work beaded brick stitch around the outer edge, over the join.

Tie the red and white striped ribbon into a bow and stitch to the edge of the circle at the base of the hanging loop. Trim the tails at an angle.

FOLK ART BIRD ORNAMENT

CHRISTMAS WREATH BY DI VAN NIEKERK

Designer:	Project:	Technique:
Di van Niekerk	Christmas wreath	Mixed media
Country of Origin:	**Fabric:**	**Threads:**
South Africa	Silk habutai and organza	Knitting yarn, silk ribbon, stranded cotton and beads
Dimensions:		**Design Transfer Required:** YES ☒ NO ☐
17.5cm x 17cm wide (6⅞" x 6¾")		

- - - - -

DESCRIPTION

A delicate Christmas wreath worked within an embroidery hoop to be hung on a wall or in a window.

- - - - -

DESIGN NOTES

A translucent window is cut from the centre of the silk fabric, creating interest in the background, which is then surrounded with a fine circlet of stems, leaves and berries, further embellished with bugle and seed beads using a traditional Christmas palette of red and green.

- - - - -

TECHNIQUE NOTES

Hand-dyed silk ribbon is used to wrap the outer hoop, providing a strongly coloured frame for the design. Layers of white silk organza and habutai are used as a base for the embroidery. Textured knitting yarns are couched on the fabric surface to create the wreath base then topped with wooden and glass beads of various sizes. Elegant leaves are worked in surface stitching and curve gracefully away from the inner and outer edges of the circle.

Wreaths

During the 8th century wreaths of ivy, laurel, oak, wheat, olive and grape vines were used by Etruscan rulers as crowns. Members of Greco-Roman society would fashion ring-shaped decorations, known as coronas, from fresh twigs, branches and leaves, small fruits and flowers. These were worn around the head to signify rank, occupation and achievements. In 16th century Germany, Lutherans hung Advent wreaths on doors that were made from the branches of evergreen bushes and trees and included four candles, one for each week of Advent. Contemporary wreaths can be made from natural or artificial foliage and decorated with coloured baubles, pinecones, ribbons and lights and are often hung on the front door of a home to welcome visitors. The wreath is a symbol of continued growth and eternity as it has no end.

FROM THE DESIGNER

"I wanted to make a décor piece that wasn't a lot of work because it's a Christmas decoration and most of us do not want to spend weeks working on one. But I wanted something that would become an heirloom piece to be passed on to the next generation. My sister is mad about decorating her Christmas tree every year and it is quite a ritual, taking her days to set it up with the most wonderful effect! Our Mum has passed all her Christmas decorations from the 1950s and 1960s on to my sister including the decorations from her mother (our Gran) and so my sister's tree has even more meaning to us as a family. That's why I thought I would make her a Christmas wreath so that she had an heirloom gift from me! This wreath would look lovely hanging from a mantlepiece or on a door or window. Its transparent window looks lovely when an interesting background shows through. The red beads and green leaves are the traditional Christmas colours and I am sure this will complement any room for Christmas! My sister will be passing these decorations on to her daughter one day, the fourth generation to have the tradition in her family."

CHRISTMAS
WREATH

COLOUR PALETTE

REQUIREMENTS

Fabric

25cm (10") square of white organza

25cm (10") square of white silk habutai

Supplies

15cm (6") embroidery hoop

12cm (4¾") square of firm card

2cm (¾") diameter gold ring

White sewing thread

Silk pins

A4 sheet of white paper

Fine, sharp scissors

Acid-free glue stick

Craft glue

Small paintbrush or cotton buds

Tracing paper

Fine black pen

Sharp 2B pencil

Needles

No. 18 chenille

No. 8 crewel

No. 10 crewel

Threads, Ribbons & Beads

DMC Variations *stranded cotton*

A = 4045 evergreen forest

Maxi Circulo *stranded cotton*

B = 244 rusty red

C = 936 brown

Di van Niekerk *7mm silk ribbon*

D = 24 lt pine (2 pkt)

E = 58 real red

Di van Niekerk *13mm silk ribbon*

F = 58 real red

Bouclé yarn

G = brown – 3m (3yd 12")

Fine mohair yarn

H = green – 2m (2yd 8")

4mm wood beads

I = red (20)

6mm wood beads

J = red (10)

14mm wood beads

K = red (2)

Miyuki *size 15 seed beads*

L = 3 silver-lined gold (4)

Miyuki *3mm bugle beads*

M = 3 silver-lined gold (15)

4mm bugle beads

N = lt green AB (12)

PREPARATION FOR EMBROIDERY

before you begin

See the liftout pattern for the embroidery design

We recommend that you read the complete article

All embroidery is worked with ONE strand of thread unless specified

Preparing the hoop

The outer ring of the hoop is wrapped with **D**. Using the glue stick, place a small dab of glue on the inside of the ring at the end of the wood close to the screw. Leaving a 15cm (6") tail of ribbon, wrap the ribbon around the ring, then, adding small dabs of glue along the inner ring surface, continue wrapping the ribbon, overlapping it a little as you work. Continue wrapping and applying more glue until reaching the second end. Secure the ribbon with a small dab of glue as before. Leave a 15cm (6") tail and trim away any excess ribbon. Allow to dry.

Preparing the fabrics

Neaten the edge of the organza and habutai squares using a machine zigzag or overlock stitch to prevent fraying. Matching edges, place the habutai square over the organza square and place both fabrics in the hoop with the silk uppermost. Tension both fabrics until the surface is drum tight.

Transferring the design

The design is transferred in two stages.

STAGE 1

Using the circle template in the liftout pattern, a compass or a glass with a 9.5cm (3¾") diameter, mark a 9.5cm (3¾") circle in the centre of the square of firm card using the pencil. Cut out, ensuring that the circle is smooth. Use fine sandpaper to sand the edges if necessary.

On a smooth, flat surface, turn the hoop over so that the organza is uppermost. Centre the card circle over the organza and trace around the circle with the pencil. Turn to the right side. Pin or baste the excess fabric at each corner out of the way.

Stage 2 is worked once the wreath base is complete.

STAGE 2

Using the fine black pen, trace the wreath design onto tracing paper. Trim the paper so that it will fit inside the hoop. Align the dot at the top of the design with the hoop screw and the design with the wreath base. Using a lid or tracing disc to support the design and fabric, trace the outer leaves onto the habutai and the inner leaves onto the organza using the pencil.

CHRISTMAS WREATH

EMBROIDERY

Refer to the close-up photograph for colour placement.

Use the no. 8 crewel needle for two strands of thread, the no. 10 crewel for one strand and the no. 18 chenille needle for the mohair yarn and ribbon.

All embroidery is worked in the hoop.

Order of work

WREATH BASE

Using two strands of **A**, work small back stitches around the marked circle through both fabrics.

> **NOTE:** If you have difficulty seeing the circle, place a piece of white paper on your worktable or lap. Take care to hold the hoop by the ring and avoid touching the fabrics as this will loosen the tension.

Using the small, sharp scissors, insert the tip of one blade between the two fabric layers just inside the back stitch circle. Carefully cut away the habutai inside the circle.

Fold a 2m (2yd 8") length of **G** in half. Find the centre of the folded yarn, position on the back stitch circle and couch in place using **C**. Lay each half of the doubled yarn over the back stitch line, forming a soft zigzag, until the tails meet, forming a circle. Couch the yarn in place at approximately 13mm (½") intervals, working each stitch over the back stitch line and using a gentle tension (fig 1).

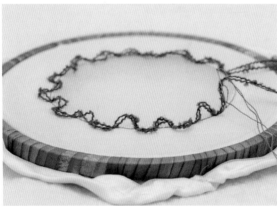

FIG 1

With the remaining tails of yarn, arrange them around the circle again, softening the zigzag a little, and couch in place as before. Continue couching the tails around the circle until all the bouclé is used (fig 2).

FIG 2

Tuck the raw ends under the wreath and couch in place. Transfer the remaining design following Stage 2.

LEAVES

Using two strands of **A**, outline one leaf with back stitch. Beginning at the tip with a detached chain, cover the leaf with close fly stitch and embroider the leaf vein and stem with stem stitch using the same thread, working the stem to the back stitch line. Scatter three-wrap French knots along the inner and outer edges of the wreath with the excess thread.

Work the remaining leaves in the same manner (fig 3).

FIG 3

Outer leaves

Using **B**, work three, two-wrap French knots at the tip of each leaf, work the leaf veins with straight stitch and whip the leaf stem using the same thread.

Inner leaves

Using **B**, attach an **M** bead at the tip of each leaf, work the leaf veins with straight stitch, attach an **L** bead at the base of the leaf and whip the stem using the same thread.

GREEN WREATH STEMS

Thread the 2m (2d 8") length of **H** into the chenille needle. Bring the thread to the surface under the wreath base. Using a gentle tension, wrap the mohair yarn around the wreath base, taking the needle to the back every 1.5cm (⅝"). Continue around the wreath, using the photograph as a guide to placement.

RED BERRIES

Using two strands of **B**, attach the **I** and **J** beads around the wreath, working two stitches through each bead and adding one **J** bead then two **I** beads around the circle. Add two-wrap French knots around the wreath using the same thread.

WREATH BUGLE BEADS

Using **A**, attach **M** and **N** beads around the wreath, angling each one towards the edge of the wreath and using the **N** beads in the upper right and lower left quarters and the **M** beads in the remaining two quarters.

FINISHING

Remove the pins or basting holding the excess fabric at each corner and press carefully using the silk setting on the iron.

Turn the hoop over so that the organza is uppermost and, leaving a 6mm (¼") seam allowance, trim away the excess organza from around the edge of the hoop.

> **HINT:** Before applying the glue to the hoop ring, cut a circle of white paper to fit exactly inside the inner hoop. Place the paper over the back of the embroidery to protect the fabric. Leave the paper in place until the glue has dried.

Using a small brush or cotton bud, carefully apply a thin layer of glue to the upper edge of the inner ring of the hoop. Allow the glue to dry slightly then press the organza seam allowance firmly onto the glued ring, clipping the seam allowance where necessary (fig 4).

FIG 4

Hold in place with clips or pegs until dry.

Leaving a 1cm (⅜") seam allowance, trim away the excess habutai from around the edge of the hoop. Using a small brush or cotton bud, carefully apply a thin layer of glue to the upper edge and upper half of the inner edge of the inner ring of the hoop. Allow the glue to dry a little then press the habutai seam allowance firmly onto the upper and inner surfaces of the glued ring, clipping the seam allowance where necessary. Hold in place with clips or pegs until dry.

Cut a length of **E** to fit inside the inner ring plus 1cm (⅜").

Using the glue stick, apply a thin layer of glue to one side of the ribbon. Press the ribbon around the inner edge of the inner ring, overlapping the ends, and hold in place with the pins until dry. Remove the paper circle.

Tie one **K** bead onto the end of each green ribbon tail. Thread the gold ring onto one tail and tie the tails together. Tie the **F** ribbon into a bow and attach at the top of the hoop.

WHITE CHRISTMAS BY DI KIRCHNER

OVERVIEW

Designer:	Project:	Technique:
Di Kirchner	Hanging ornament with holly	Three-dimensional embroidery
Country of Origin:	**Fabric:**	**Threads:**
Australia	Cotton	Stranded rayon, metallic thread

Dimensions:	
10cm (4") in diameter	Design Transfer Required: YES ☒ NO ☐

DESCRIPTION

Large hanging ornament with holly and berries in shades of grey and white.

DESIGN NOTES

Holly leaves, clusters of large and small berries, beaded twigs and curling tendrils are gathered at the base of a large ring. Rays of metallic thread emanate from the berries and foliage and organza ribbon forms a hanging loop and decorative bow.

TECHNIQUE NOTES

Three-dimensional leaves, berries, stems and tendrils are created using stumpwork techniques and a combination of rayon, cotton and metallic threads. Large beads are wrapped with thread then covered with seed beads to form the large berries while pebble beads are wrapped to create the holly berries. The metal ring is covered with close blanket stitch, forming a base through which the metallic thread rays are worked.

White Christmas

Written by Irving Berlin for the 1942 American film, Holiday Inn, and sung by Bing Crosby, the Academy Award winning White Christmas is the world's best-selling single, having sold more than fifty million copies. Coupled with sales of the song released by other artists, sales have exceeded one hundred million copies. There have been more than five hundred recorded versions of the song, including ones by Ella Fitzgerald, Otis Redding, Michael Bublé and Taylor Swift. Berlin is thought to have written the song while staying in sunny California and he believed at the time that it was the best song he had ever written. Bing Crosby first performed it on a radio program on Christmas Day 1941 and he later recorded it on an album of six, 78 rpm discs for the film. His recording spent eleven weeks on the top of the Billboard charts and established the potential commercial success of Christmas songs. The version now usually heard was recorded in 1947 as the 1942 master copy was damaged by overuse and every effort was made to reproduce the original, although additional musical instruments were used.

FROM THE DESIGNER

"When deciding what Christmas decoration I would design, the first thing that came into my mind was that I wanted it to be pretty and delicate. I visualised something white.

I started working with the idea of a wreath that could hang on a wall or door. It soon became evident that this project idea would be immense. So, when downscaling my design, the idea of a window or tree decoration seemed more achievable.

The embroidery technique I chose to achieve my idea was stumpwork. The three-dimensional effect of stumpwork enabled me to create a wreath with leaves, berries and twigs on a thread-covered metal ring. By adding the silver thread and beads to the design it sparkled more in the light.

My main inspiration came from photos on the internet, the magic of a White Christmas and the love of pretty things".

WHITE CHRISTMAS

COLOUR PALETTE

REQUIREMENTS

Fabric

20cm (8") square of white cotton

Supplies

15cm (6") embroidery hoop

36cm (14") lengths of 28 gauge white paper-covered wire (4)

36cm (14") lengths of 33 gauge white paper-covered wire (10)

12mm (¹⁵⁄₃₂") wooden barrel beads (3)

10cm (4") galvanised metal craft ring

80cm x 13mm wide (32" x ½") white bias binding

1.5m x 25mm wide (1yd 23" x 1") white organza ribbon

Fine sharp embroidery scissors

Scissors to cut wire

Needle-nose pliers

Craft glue

Tracing paper

Fine black pen

Fine heat-soluble fabric marker

Needles

No. 6 crewel

No. 9 crewel

No. 9 milliner's

Threads & Beads

Anchor Marlitt *stranded rayon*
A = 800 snow white

Au Papillion Fil d'Or Deluxe *metallic thread*
B = dk silver

DMC *no. 16 floche*
C = blanc
D = 415 pearl grey

DMC Light Effects *stranded metallic*
E = E168 silver

DMC *no. 5 perlé cotton*
F = B5200 snow white

DMC *no. 12 perlé cotton*
G = B5200 snow white

DMC *stranded cotton*
H = B5200 snow white

Madeira Decora *stranded rayon*
I = 1410 lt grey

Mill Hill *seed beads*
J = 02010 ice (10)

Mill Hill *pebble beads*
K = 05021 silver (10)

Ribtex *1.8mm seed beads*
L = SB060 white

Pearl beads 4mm
M = white (20)

this design uses

Beading, p214

Blanket stitch, p214

Couching, p214

Satin stitch, p215

Straight stitch, p215

Wrapping

before you begin

See the liftout pattern for the leaf template

We recommend that you read the complete article

All embroidery is worked with ONE strand of thread

PREPARATION FOR EMBROIDERY

Preparing the fabric

Neaten the raw edges of the cotton square with a machine zigzag or overlock stitch to prevent fraying.

Transferring the design

Using the black pen, trace the leaf template onto tracing paper. Tape the tracing to a lightbox or window. Centre the inner ring of the 15cm (6") hoop onto the fabric. Using the heat-soluble fabric marker, trace around the inner edge of the ring to mark a circle. Working within the marked circle, transfer the shaping for six leaves using the heat-soluble fabric marker. Place the fabric into the embroidery hoop and tension until drum tight, taking care not to distort the shapes.

- - - - -

EMBROIDERY

Refer to the close-up photograph for colour and stitch placement.

Use the no. 6 crewel needle for the no. 5 perlé cotton, the no. 9 crewel for the leaf embroidery and the no. 9 milliner's needle for wrapping and attaching beads.

The leaf embroidery is worked in the hoop.

Order of work

LEAVES

Leaving a 6cm (2⅜") tail at each end, couch a length of 33 gauge wire around one leaf shape using **A**. Using the same thread, cover the wire outline with close blanket stitch.

Using **C**, fill each half of the leaf with satin stitch, angling the stitches towards the tip. Using **E**, embroider the centre vein with one long straight stitch approximately three-quarters of the length of the leaf and couch at three, evenly spaced intervals. Using the same thread, work pairs of side veins with straight stitch so that the base of each pair is aligned with a couching stitch along the centre vein. Embroider the remaining five leaves in the same manner.

When all leaf embroidery is complete, carefully cut out using the fine, sharp embroidery scissors and following the step-by-step instructions on page 207. Secure a length of **G** on the wrong side of one leaf near the base and use it to wrap the wire tails together to the end to form a stem. Secure the thread with a half hitch and leave the thread tail for construction. Repeat to make wrapped stems for the remaining five leaves.

WHITE CHRISTMAS

PEARL TWIGS

Thread one **M** bead onto a length of 33 gauge wire and position at the centre. Fold the wire in half, bringing the tails together directly beneath the bead. Thread a long length of **G** through the bead, so that you have a long and short tail. Tie the thread tails together beneath the bead.

Holding the wires and short thread tail together and referring to diagram 1, use the long tail to wrap them together for 2cm (¾"). Bend one wire tail up at a 45 degree angle. Thread on an **M** bead and fold the wire back down to create a 1.5cm (⅝") twig. Thread a new length of **G** through the bead, secure and wrap back to the centre twig in the same manner as before. Lay the thread tail down the centre twig. Repeat to form a second wire twig with the second wire tail. Using the first thread tail, continue to wrap the wires and thread tails for 8mm (⁵⁄₁₆"). Form two side twigs in the same manner as before. Continue wrapping the centre twig for 1.5cm (⅝"), incorporating the thread tails. Secure the wrapping thread with one or two half hitches and do not cut (diag 1).

GREY TENDRILS

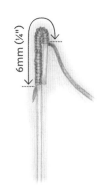

Cut four, 23cm (9") lengths of 28 gauge wire. Tie a long length of **D** 1cm (⅜") from the end of one length of wire, leaving one short tail and one very long tail of thread. Using the long tail, tightly wrap the wire, for 6mm (¼") towards the tip. Fold the 1cm (⅜") section in half so that the fold is just before the end of the wrapping (diag 2).

Carefully squeeze the loop closed with the needle-nose pliers and continue wrapping tightly down away from the folded tip incorporating the short tail.

Continue wrapping the wire to the end and secure the thread with a half-hitch. Do not cut the thread tail. Leaving 4cm–5cm (1½"–2") at the lower end straight, gently wrap the remaining length around a pencil to create the tendril.

Repeat with the remaining three lengths of wire.

SMALL SILVER BERRIES

Leaving a 10cm (4") tail, tie a long length of **I** to a **K** bead and adjust so that the knot is inside the bead. Taking the thread up through the bead each time, wrap the bead until the surface is covered, keeping the wraps as smooth as possible. When the bead is completely covered, take the thread through the centre to the top of the bead, thread on a **J** bead and take the thread back down through the centre of the **K** bead to the base. Trim the thread to leave a second, 10cm (4") tail. Repeat to make a total of ten small berries.

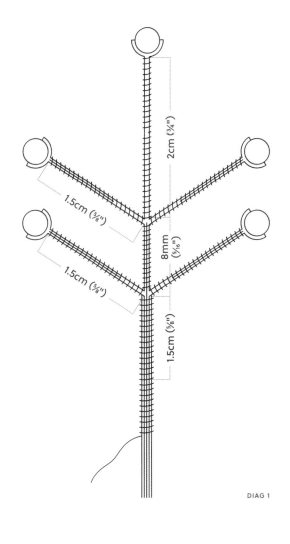

DIAG 1

LARGE WHITE BERRIES

Using **H**, wrap each of the three wooden beads in a similar manner to the small silver berries, omitting the bead at the tip. Using the same thread, stitch **L** beads to the wrapping of each wooden bead. Attach the **L** beads securely, one or two at a time, until the surface is completely covered.

RING

Press the folds of the bias binding open with an iron. Wrap the metal ring with the tape, overlapping the wraps by half. When reaching the starting point, secure the tape with a few small stitches using **H**. Using **F**, cover the wrapped ring with close blanket stitch, keeping the beaded edge of the stitching along the outer edge of the ring. Secure the thread tails under the stitching on the wrong side.

SILVER RAYS

The silver rays are worked through the inner edge of the ring, beginning and returning to the centre base. Referring to the diagram, secure a very long length of **B** under the stitching and emerge at the centre of the lower inner edge of the ring. Take the needle under a blanket stitch 5mm (³⁄₁₆") to the left of the upper centre, again on the inner edge of the ring. Pull the thread through. Return to the base, anchor the thread at the centre and pull the thread through to complete the first ray. Work a further seven rays at 1cm (⅜") intervals to the same side as the first ray, spreading the anchoring stitches at the centre base slightly as needed. Work a ninth ray to the same side 1.5cm (⅜") from the last ray. Work nine rays as a mirror image, spacing each the same distance apart, beginning 5mm (³⁄₁₆") to the right of the upper centre (diag 3).

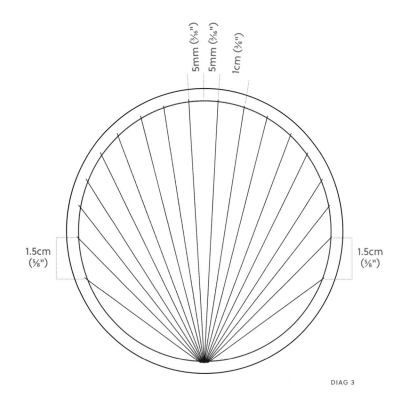

DIAG 3

- - - - -

CONSTRUCTION

Preparing the sprays

Cut a length of **G**. Place three leaves together in a fan shape, staggering the positions and ensuring that the tip of the centre leaf extends furthest out. Position the stems of two grey tendrils behind the leaf stems, fanning them slightly. Position two pearl twigs over the leaves, fanning them slightly and adjusting as desired.

Working 1cm (⅜") below the base of the lowest leaf in the group, secure the length of **G** around the bundle of wires and thread tails with a half hitch. Tightly wrap the bundle for 2cm (¾") and secure with a small dab of glue. Do not cut the thread. Trim the wires to the desired length so that the ends are even.

Cut six, 6mm (¼") lengths of **G**. Apply a small amount of glue to the end of the wires and glue three of the lengths over the ends then the remaining three over the ends perpendicular to the first group (diag 4).

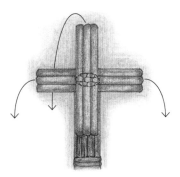

Using the wrapping thread, wrap to the end of the stem, ensuring that all the wire is covered. Secure the wrapping thread with a half hitch knot and run the tail a short distance under the wraps using the no. 6 crewel needle. Add a small dab of glue. Allow to dry and trim away the excess thread.

Repeat to form a spray with the remaining leaves, grey tendrils and pearl twigs.

Preparing the small silver berries

Form a cluster with five berries. Using a thread tail from the group, wrap all thread tails together at the base of the cluster and stitch through the tails and wrapping a few times. Repeat to form a cluster with the remaining five berries.

Attaching the sprays and berries

Position the sprays over the base of the ring, crossing the wrapped stems. Bind the stems to the ring by wrapping securely using **G**. Push the ends of the stems up to follow the curve of the ring. Arrange the large berries and small berry clusters and bind to the stems and ring by wrapping using the thread tails and **G**.

Hanging loop and bow

Using the organza ribbon, make a hanging loop and bow at the centre top of the ring. Trim the bow tails as desired.

MEMORIES
BY
MARGARET LEE

OVERVIEW

Designer:	Project:	Technique:
Margaret Lee	Beaded mat	Japanese-style bead embroidery
Country of Origin:	**Fabric:**	**Threads:**
Australia	Silk taffeta	Beading threads and beads

Dimensions:	**Design Transfer Required:** YES [X] NO [ ]
28cm x 38cm wide (11" x 15")	

- - - - -

DESCRIPTION

Ornate beaded rectangular table centre in festive shades of red and gold worked onto silk taffeta.

- - - - -

DESIGN NOTES

The quartered design surrounds a centre circle stitched with metal thread, allowing the addition of a candle or vase. The bauble at each corner is painted with gold before the beading commences.

- - - - -

TECHNIQUE NOTES

Japanese-style bead embroidery is based on concepts of traditional Japanese embroidery. Unlike other styles of bead embroidery, seed beads are used almost exclusively and traditional techniques underpin the practice. Meticulous attention to detail and application in different design situations make this style unique.

Glass beads

The story of glass beads goes back to around 2400 BC and throughout history they have played an important role in many cultures across the globe. Often representing wealth, power and spirituality, they have been used as adornment in ceremonies and rituals and exchanged as currency. Early examples were made in Asia, Mesopotamia and Egypt and between 400 BC and 100 BC, the Romans manufactured and traded with beads across their empire. The Vikings ran sophisticated bead-making operations between the 8th and 11th centuries in Scandinavia and by the Middle Ages, glass seed beads were being made in Italy, initially in Venice then in Murano. Developing techniques for mass producing beads, the Italians held a monopoly on the industry for around 600 years. By the 19th century most of the production had moved to Bohemia and the best beads are now manufactured in the Czech Republic and Japan.

FROM THE DESIGNER

When we remember a special Christmas, it is not the presents that made it special, but the laughter, the feeling of love, and the togetherness of friends and family that made that Christmas special.

CATHERINE PULSIFER

"How true indeed! Our annual Christmas gathering for dinner on Christmas Eve involves just that with trips down memory lane of Christmas past as well as loved ones no longer with us.

A table centrepiece had been on the 'to-do' embroidery list for some time. In my mind's eye, it will grace the table on special occasions and become part of a family tradition. This seems to be the right time to activate the plan and produce a centrepiece for the Christmas table.

Embroidery designs in our culture often hold special meaning. I wished for this centrepiece to do the same and started by jotting down design elements that embody the spirit of Christmas.

- The festive table with family and friends gathered round.

- The Christmas star that retells the Christmas story and the special gift through the birth of Jesus Christ.

- Baubles, tinsel, decorations, and fairy lights that gaily decorate the Christmas tree.

The design was beginning to take shape in the mind's eye but, somehow, something was still missing. A souvenir candle holder in the shape of a snow crystal from a family holiday to Finland provided the final design element.

- The central round pattern symbolises the unbroken bond of family and friends around the festive table. Arranged around this circle are flame shaped elements symbolising the warmth of love and friendship.

- The centre circle is stitched with metallic threads to keep a flat surface as I envisaged a pillar candle, or a vase of flowers placed in that space.

- The Christmas star and snow crystals speak their own Christmas message. To create the colour spectrum that glistens off real snow crystals, 3-cut transparent lustre beads were selected and stitched with a multi-colour silver/blue metallic thread.

- The corner design of the mat incorporates a Christmas bauble along with small flowers and leaf patterns strung together by a line stitched with gold metallic threads. These represent festive decorations of the season.

- Finally, what is Christmas without fairy lights. These are incorporated into the design with alternate gold lustered beads, in green and orange/gold, around the edges of the mat and along the outline of the corner shape.

I hope you enjoy this Christmas mat as much as I have in creating it."

MEMORIES

COLOUR PALETTE

MEMORIES

MEMORIES

REQUIREMENTS

Fabric

48cm x 38cm wide (19" x 15") piece of scarlet silk taffeta

Supplies

Slate frame to fit fabric

Lacing thread

50wt off-white cotton sewing thread

50wt red cotton sewing thread

30cm x 40cm wide (12" x 16") piece of adhesive felt

30cm x 40cm wide (12" x 16") piece of adhesive vinyl

Jacquard Lumiere metallic gold acrylic paint

Small paint brush

Pair of koma

Tekobari or laying tool

Silk pins

Craft glue

Green or blue dressmaker's carbon

Ruler

Stylus or spent ballpoint pen

Tracing paper

Fine black pen

Needles

No. 22 chenille

No. 7 sharp

No. 10 sharp

No. 11 sharp

No. 12 sharp

Threads & beads

Japanese metal threads
A = no. 1 gold – 10m (11yd)

B = no. 1 silver-blue multi-colour metallic – 18m (19yd 24")

C = no. 3 twisted silver – 16m (17yd 24")

Superior Kimono *no. 100 silk*
D = 377 Ginza

BEADS

Bead quantities listed refer to a 5cm x 12mm (2" x ½") tube

Czech fire polished beads 2mm
E = bronze (44pc)

Czech fire polished beads 4mm
F = bronze (16pc)

Preciosa *size 9 3-cut beads*
G = emerald lustre (⅔)

Preciosa *size 12 3-cut beads*
H = green iris (⅔)

Toho size 11 seed beads
I = 322 gold lustre teal green (½)

J = 329 gold lustre African sunset (½)

K = 551 galvanised rose gold (5)

L = 557 galvanised starlight gold (¼)

M = 558 galvanised aluminium (3)

N = 564 galvanised brick red (1¼)

O = 594 galvanised bronze (½)

Toho size 15 seed beads
P = 5C transparent ruby (5)

Q = 322 gold lustre teal green (¼)

R = 329 gold lustre African sunset (¼)

S = 221 bronze metallic (¼)

T = 241 rainbow lt topaz/mauve-lined (1¼)

U = 551 galvanised rose-gold (¼)

V = 557 galvanised starlight gold (1 ½)

W = 558 galvanised aluminium (¾)

X = 564 galvanised brick red (¾)

Toho size 12 3-cut beads
Y = 101 transparent lustre crystal (½)

Z = 557 galvanised starlight gold (¼)

AA = 558 galvanised aluminium (1)

Toho size 15 3-cut beads
AB = 101 transparent lustre crystal (½)

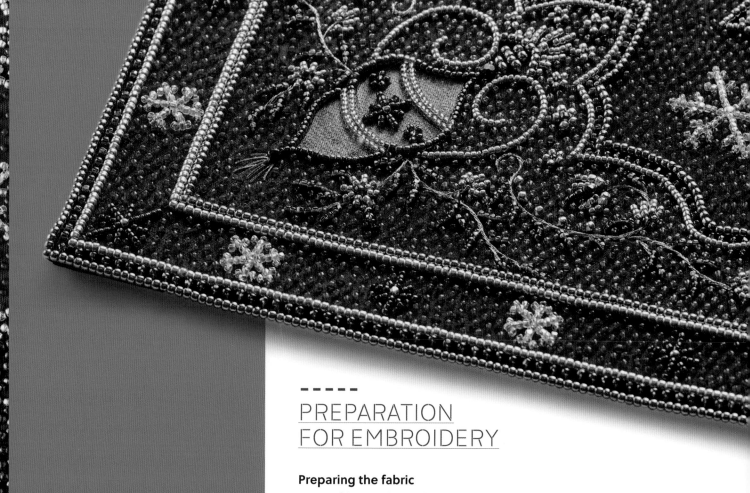

before you begin

See the liftout pattern for the embroidery design

We recommend that you read the complete article

PREPARATION FOR EMBROIDERY

Preparing the fabric

Using a fabric marker or thread, mark the warp edges of the fabric on the wrong side.

Transferring the design

Using the black pen trace the design and border lines onto tracing paper. Place the fabric, right side uppermost, on a firm surface. Centre the design over the fabric and pin in place along one long edge. Slide a piece of dressmaker's carbon, chalk side down, under the tracing paper and pin in place well outside the design area. Using the stylus and ruler and pressing firmly, re-trace the design and border lines. Check to ensure that the lines have transferred successfully before removing the carbon. Work a line of running stitch around the rectangle, 1mm (1/32") out from the outer border line using the off-white sewing thread and working long stitches on the right side and very short stitches on the wrong side (diag 1).

Fold under 1cm (3/8") on each side of the fabric and press. Ensuring that the warp edges of the fabric run along the upper and lower edges, place the fabric into the frame, tensioning until the surface is tight. Check to ensure that the border lines have not been distorted by the framing process. Adjust if necessary.

Painting the baubles

Using the paint brush and metallic gold paint, carefully paint the three sections of each bauble with a thin layer. Allow to dry.

MEMORIES

BEADING

Refer to the close-up photograph for colour placement.

Use the no. 22 chenille needle for the twisted metal thread, the no. 7 sharp needle for the no. 1 metal threads and construction, the no. 10 sharp for couching, the no. 12 sharp for the no. 15 beads and the no. 11 sharp for all other beads.

All embroidery is worked in the frame.

Order of work

> **NOTE:** Japanese-style bead embroidery is worked with two needles, one with a doubled thread that is used to lay the beads or attach single beads, and one with a single thread that is used to couch the line of beads in place.

Use the off-white sewing thread for all beaded motifs unless specified and the red sewing thread for attaching the background beads and construction.

> **Pin stitch - Beginning, ending and securing threads**
>
> Pin stitch is the name given to the tiny back stitches that are used in Japanese-style bead embroidery. Threads are started with a knot and two pin stitches and the thread is then brought to the fabric surface ready to begin the work. Threads are finished with three pin stitches and the thread is brought to the fabric surface and cut away.
>
> When the distance between two areas of beading is more than 1cm (⅜") or it is necessary to secure beads, one or two pin stitches are worked to secure the thread before moving it to the next working area. Do not cut the thread.
>
> All pin stitches should be worked in an area that is to be covered by beads or beneath existing beads. Once each element is complete work a pin stitch with each needle to secure the thread before moving to the next element.

CENTRE MOTIF

Using *couching technique 1: needle-koma method*, couch a line of **AA** beads along the outer edge of the circle.

Couch six rows of pairs of **C** around the inner edge of the circle using **D** and *couching technique: 1 pair inward coil method*.

Work the outer line of the ogee pattern using *couching technique 1: needle-koma method* in the following manner. Bring the needle up in a valley and thread on the required number of **K** and three **U**. Take the needle to the back one point past the tip of the shape. Bring the needle up in the next valley and thread on the

required number of **K** and two **U**. Take the needle to the back through the last bead at the tip. Continue working in this manner around the edge.

Work the inner line of the ogee pattern in a similar manner using the required number of **N**.

> **Couching technique 1: Needle-koma method**
>
> Bring the thread to the front at one end of the line. Thread on the required number of beads. Wind the excess thread and needle onto the koma. Beginning at the first bead and using a second needle with a single strand of thread couch the line at two-bead intervals. Tension after working each couching stitch by tugging on the koma. Keeping the thread under tension use the koma to position the line of beads for the next couching stitch. Continue working in this manner to the end of the line. Unwind the thread and take it to the back at the end of the line. Tension the thread and work a pin stitch to secure.

> **Couching technique: 1 pair inward coil method**
>
> For the circle in this project, couching stitches are just under 2mm (¹⁄₁₆") apart. Identify any point along the circumference of the circle. Commence with a couching stitch over one thread (thread A) at this point and follow with another two stitches. Add the second thread (thread B) on the inside and couch over the pair of threads. Continue to couch the pair along the circle shape for another four stitches. Sink the ends of both threads at the points where the respective first couching commenced for each. Brick the couching and continue around the circle for six rows.
>
> End the couching as follows:
>
> 1. End Thread A first at the point that lines up with where the thread started. Sink the end just beyond the last couching stitch.
>
> 2. Continue with Thread B until it aligns with the start also. Note that these last few stitches should be over two threads, which means that the couching is over this thread and the adjoining thread from the previous row. Sink as above (fig 1).

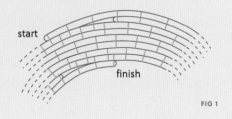

start

finish

FIG 1

Fill the area between the inner and outer lines with single stitches using three **W** at the point of the valley and two **W** in the remaining areas.

Work the group of radiating stitches at the base of each ogee shape in the following manner. Make the centre stitch using two **S**, one **O**, one **E**, one **F** and one **E**. Work three diagonal stitches on each side of the centre, beginning with the stitch at the base and working towards the centre. Stitch from the outer edge to the base using three **V** and three **Z** for the first stitch, three **V**, two **Z** and one **V** for the second stitch and five **V** for the third stitch, couching in place as necessary to shape.

Fill the background with *scatter effect – singles technique* using **N** and **X** in the tapered areas, and red sewing thread.

Scatter effect – singles technique

Stitch single beads randomly in the space to be filled keeping the space between the beads consistent and ensuring that they are facing different directions and do not form lines. The background fabric should show through.

Snowflake

Beginning at one corner, couch three rows of pairs of **C** around the outer hexagon using **D**, working from the outside towards the centre. Stitch each long arm with two stitches using **C**, couched down with **D** using *line of held thread technique*.

Stitch right across the shape, taking the threads under the outer hexagon, working both stitches before commencing the couching over both threads. Work the side branches in the same manner.

Line of held thread technique

This technique is used to couch any stitch or pair of stitches along a straight or curved design line. Begin with a stitch from end to end of the design line. Work a couching stitch at the centre of the line. Continue working couching stitches at the midpoints of the divided sections of thread until the stitching interval is no less than 1cm (⅜").

Stitch the inner hexagon in the same manner, working two stitches between each long arm.

Embroider the short arms with single stitches, working under the hexagons and centre and couching **C** with **D**.

CORNER MOTIF OUTLINE

Each corner outline is worked in the same manner.

Work the outer line with *couching technique 1: needle-koma method* using **K** and a single **U** bead at the centre point. Work the inner line in a similar manner using **W**.

Stitch single beads between the two lines, beginning at the centre point and alternating **Q** and **R**. The hole of each bead should be perpendicular to the border.

CENTRE MOTIF BACKGROUND

Large snowflakes

The large snowflakes are worked using **Y**, **AB** and **B** with the lines of beads couched down with white thread.

Stitch the first two arms of the snowflake as one continuous line using *line of held thread technique: beading* with several **AB** at each end of the line.

Line of held thread technique: Beading

This technique is used to create linear effects by holding stitches in place along a line with couched stitches. It is usually used for relatively short lines.

Bring the needle with the doubled thread up at one end of the line. Thread on the required number of beads. Take the needle to the back at the other end of the line. Secure the second needle with the single thread and bring it to the front at the centre of the line. Work a couching stitch at this point. Continue working couching stitches at least two beads apart. Couch between every bead if a firm line is required.

Work the remaining arms to the centre of the snowflake in a similar manner with **AB** at the outer edge. Stitch each small branch as a single stitch using 2–3 **AB**.

Small snowflakes

The small snowflakes are worked in a similar manner to the large snowflakes using **AB** and one **Y** at the centre of the first two arms, and **AB** for the remaining arms and branches.

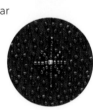

Stars

Stitch the long, vertical arm of each star using six **X**, one **L** or **Z** and six **X** using the *line of held thread technique: beading*. Work each horizontal arm with a single stitch using four **X** and couching between each bead. Work each diagonal arm in the same manner using three **X**.

Background

Fill the background with *scatter effect – singles technique* using **P** and the red sewing thread.

CORNER

Each corner is worked in the same manner.

Bauble

The bauble is outlined in two sections using *couching technique 1: needle-koma method*.

INNER SECTION

Begin at the tip with one **F** and the required number of **S** to reach down one side to the first band. Add two **V**, the required number of **O** and one **S** to reach the top of the second band. Add the required number of **V** to reach across the inner edge of the second band to the second side. Work back to the tip with beads in the reverse order to the first side – one **S**, the required number of **O** to reach the first band, two **V** and the required number of **S** to reach the first **S** on the first side. Take the needle back through the first **S** on the first side and the **F** at the tip. Take the needle to the back through the same hole as the first stitch.

OUTER SECTION

Begin at the tip with one **E** and the required number of **S** to reach down one side to the second band. Add enough **V** to reach across the outer edge of the second band to the second side. Work back to the tip with the required number of **S** to reach the second **S** on the first side. Take the needle back through the two **S** on the first side and the **E** at the tip. Take the needle to the back through the same hole as the first stitch. Work radiating straight stitches of various lengths from the tip using two strands of **A**.

FIRST BAND

Stitch the first band with two rows of **V** using *couching technique 1: needle-koma method*.

Work the star between the two bands in the same manner as the background stars with four **X**, one **L** or **Z** and four **X** for the long, vertical arm, using *line of held thread technique: beading*. Work each horizontal arm with a single stitch using three **V** and couching between each bead. Work each diagonal arm in the same manner using two **X**. Stitch a five-petal flower on each side of the star using a **V** for the centre and **X** for the petals (fig 2).

FIG 2

CURVING LINES

Work the curved line of beads on each side of the bauble using *couching technique 1: needle-koma method*. Begin at the side of the bauble with the required number of **W** to complete the line. Stitch the arc between the lines using **K** and work three, short lines beneath the arc using the same beads. Attach one **M** at the centre of the arc then work radiating lines on each side in the following manner. Work a single vertical stitch and two side stitches of four **V** that are angled towards the centre bead. Add three stitches on each side with **V** using four for the first stitch, two for the second stitch and one bead for the third stitch.

LEAVES

Work each leaf with a single stitch using **G** and **H** and *line of held thread technique: beading*. Stitch the finer leaves with only **H** and the remainder with **G** and **H**, using **H** at the ends of each stitch. Once all leaves are complete, work the stems with *line of staggered diagonals technique* (stem stitch) using two strands of **A**. Attach five evenly spaced **M** or **AA** beads along the inner section of the upper stems.

SMALL SIDE-FACING FLOWERS

Stitch the centre of the larger flowers with a single stitch using two **S**, one **O** and two **E**, working from the petal tip to the base. Stitch the side petals in a similar manner

Line of staggered diagonals technique (fig 3)

All stitching must be done so that the stitch progression follows a clockwise direction.

a) Begin with a stitch half the desired stitch length.

b) Work a second stitch beginning to the immediate right of the first stitch at the same level. This stitch is twice the length of the first stitch and is the full stitch length.

c) The third stitch is the full stitch length and commences halfway up the previous stitch.

d) Repeat step (c) to the end of the line.

e) The final stitch is a half length stitch to complete the sequence.

FIG 3

using two **V** and two **L** for the outer petals and four **V** for the inner petals. Couch between the beads as required to shape the lines.

Stitch the centre of the smaller flowers with a single stitch using three **V** and one **H**, working from the petal tip to the base. Work two petals on one side of the centre and one on the second side using three **V**. Couch between the beads as required to shape the lines.

SMALL ROUND FLOWERS

Attach an **N** for each flower centre and stitch each petal with two **V**, working into the centre. Stitch the vertical and horizontal petals first then add the diagonal petals, couching between the beads as required.

FIVE-PETAL FLOWERS

Stitch the larger five-petal flowers using **N** for the centre and **M** or **AA** for the petals and the smaller flowers using **X** for the centre and **W** for the petals.

BACKGROUND

Stitch the background with *scatter effect – singles technique* in two steps using **T** for the areas enclosed by an inner shaped outline and the two long lower leaf stems and **P** for the areas enclosed by the two lower long leaf stems and a corner.

BORDER

Check the size of the inner marked border rectangle and adjust if necessary. Check the distance between the inner and outer marked border rectangles to ensure that the spacing is consistent and adjust if necessary.

Using *couching technique 2: long straight lines*, work the inner line of the inner border and the outer line of the outer border using **K**.

Work a second line outside the inner border in a similar manner using **M** and the inner line of the outer border, using the same beads. Stitch single beads between the two lines, approximately a bead space apart and alternating **I** and **J**.

Work a large star at each corner in the same manner as in the centre motif background. Work the small stars that alternate with the small snowflakes in the same manner as on the bauble band.

Stitch the small snowflakes using **AB** and **B**, working the first two arms of the snowflake as one continuous line using *line of held thread technique: beading* with four **AB**, one **Y** and four **AB**.

Work the remaining arms to the centre of the snowflake in a similar manner using four **AB**. Stitch each small branch as a single stitch using one **AB**. Fill the background using **P** and *scatter effect – singles technique*.

> ### Couching technique 2: Long straight lines
> Begin as for *line of held thread technique: beading* ensuring the thread length is sufficient for the line. After the first two couching stitches, extend the thread along the line to be stitched right to the end. Insert a pin through the fabric 1cm (⅜") from the end of the line and emerge at the end of the line. Wrap the thread around both ends of the pin in a figure eight motion. Maintain tension and check that the thread is exactly along the line to be stitched. Adjust if necessary. This creates a plumb line that is true and straight.
>
> Couch the line in place in the same manner as *line of held thread technique: beading*.

CONSTRUCTION

All seam allowances are 2cm (¾") unless specified. The shaded areas on the following diagrams indicate the right side of the fabric.

Preparing the beaded fabric

Do not remove the fabric from the frame. Check the tension and adjust if necessary. Check the wrong side of the fabric for stray loops or threads and secure in the following manner.

SHORT LOOPS: Thread up a needle and anchor the thread with two pin stitches at a distance 5mm (³⁄₁₆") longer than the loop. Hook the loop with the needle and thread and pull until it lies flat against the fabric. Finish with three pin stitches. All pin stitches should be hidden behind beads.

LONG LOOPS OR THREADS: If there is sufficient length, thread into a needle and secure with three pin stitches, ensuring the stitches are hidden behind beads.

Spray the wrong side with water and rub with your fingers to ensure that the moisture has penetrated all threads. Place, wrong side uppermost, in a sunny position or near a heater to dry. This will help settle the threads and fabric.

Attaching the felt backing

Measure the completed beaded piece along the outer line of beading. Using this measurement minus 1.5mm (³⁄₆₄") on each side, mark a rectangle on the adhesive felt and cut out. Check to ensure that the felt fits just inside the outer line of beading and adjust if necessary.

Peel away the adhesive backing and centre the felt over the wrong side of the embroidery, pressing gently (diag 1).

FELT

WRONG SIDE

Check to ensure that the felt is positioned correctly and adjust if necessary. The line of running stitch should be visible outside the felt. Working from the centre, apply pressure with a sweeping motion to ensure that the felt is securely fixed to the back of the embroidery.

Preparing the beaded fabric for the vinyl backing

Remove the fabric from the frame and cut out leaving a 2cm (¾") seam allowance from the line of tacking. Mitre each corner, trimming away any excess fabric, and stitch in place using the red sewing thread. Apply a thin layer of glue along each straight edge. Fold the seam allowance over, ensuring that the outer line of beads sits slightly over the edge, and press in place (diag 2).

FELT

Allow to dry.

Measure the completed beaded piece along the outer line of beading. Using this measurement minus 2mm (¹⁄₁₆") on each side, mark a rectangle on the adhesive vinyl and cut out.

Attach the vinyl in the same manner as the felt.

Remove the running stitch.

BOX OF DELIGHTS BY HELEN M. STEVENS

OVERVIEW

Designer:	Project:	Technique:
Helen M. Stevens	Wooden box with embroidered insert and small embroideries	Silk embroidery

Country of Origin:	Fabric:	Threads:
UK	Polycotton	Silk floss

Dimensions:
Embroidery measures 17.5cm (7") square,
box measures 26cm (10¼") square x 8cm (3⅛") deep,
small embroideries measure 7.5cm (3") square

Design Transfer Required: YES ☒ NO ☐

DESCRIPTION

Wooden box with inlaid lid embroidery containing three small embroideries.

DESIGN NOTES

The box embroidery features the hellebore, commonly known as the Christmas rose in the Northern Hemisphere where it is one of few plants in flower during winter and the festive season. The small designs feature sweet pea, fuchsia and morning glory flowers and each one is framed with a gold card mount.

TECHNIQUE NOTES

The embroidery is worked with multiple strands of silk floss and fine twisted silk using mainly straight stitches onto pale yellow polycotton fabric for the lid insert and black for the small embroideries. Shadow lines and voiding are used to give definition to the elements of each flower and the perceived colour of each thread varies depending on the angle of the stitches and the play of light, adding richness to the surface.

Stitching with silk floss

Silk floss differs from stranded thread in that it is made up from continuous, untwisted filaments of silk rather than short lengths that are spun and plied together. Consequently, it is much stronger and more lustrous than stranded silk and can be carefully broken down into smaller strands for very fine details. The fine filaments can catch easily on rough skin or any sharp surface so care should be taken to protect the working thread and finished embroidery from any potential hazards. The finished surface of embroidery worked with silk floss has an incomparable smoothness and lustre and the colours have a depth and richness unobtainable with other fibres.

FROM THE DESIGNER

"Most of us have a favourite Christmas book, one which we read, or had read to us as children that has stayed with us until adulthood. Often, it colours our perception of the festive season throughout our lives; scenes, characters and quotes subtly infusing themselves into our celebration, almost without our being aware ... except for that indefinable sense of childhood's Christmas magic, which we hope never to lose.

For me, that favourite books is "The Box of Delights" by John Masefield, published in 1935. It is a strange, almost surreal tale of a young boy, a Punch and Judy man (though he is much more than that), heroes and villains, set in a pre-war world, now lost to us and almost as otherworldly and beautiful as the supernatural dimension entered by the young protagonist, Kay. It is a book of layers, of things hidden and things revealed, all set in a snow-bound English village during the Christmas holidays.

When I was asked to contribute to this Design Collective title, my mind immediately went to this much-loved book. Over the years, I have worked a number of boxes, following in an ancient embroidery tradition, in spirit, if not in style. This box itself is a simple, beautifully crafted piece suitable for whatever delights you might choose to keep in it, and I have added a few little treasures to start you off! These would make delightful Christmas gifts in themselves.

When Masefield's Box was opened 'It was lit from within and multitudinous, tiny things were shifting there... "It's all alive and it's full of summer," Kay said.' Around Christmas time I always begin to pine for the summer – and so the treasures in our box reflect those that Kay found. In the traditional, Language of Flowers, they represent beauty, summer love and blissful delight."

COLOUR PALETTE

BOX OF
DELIGHTS

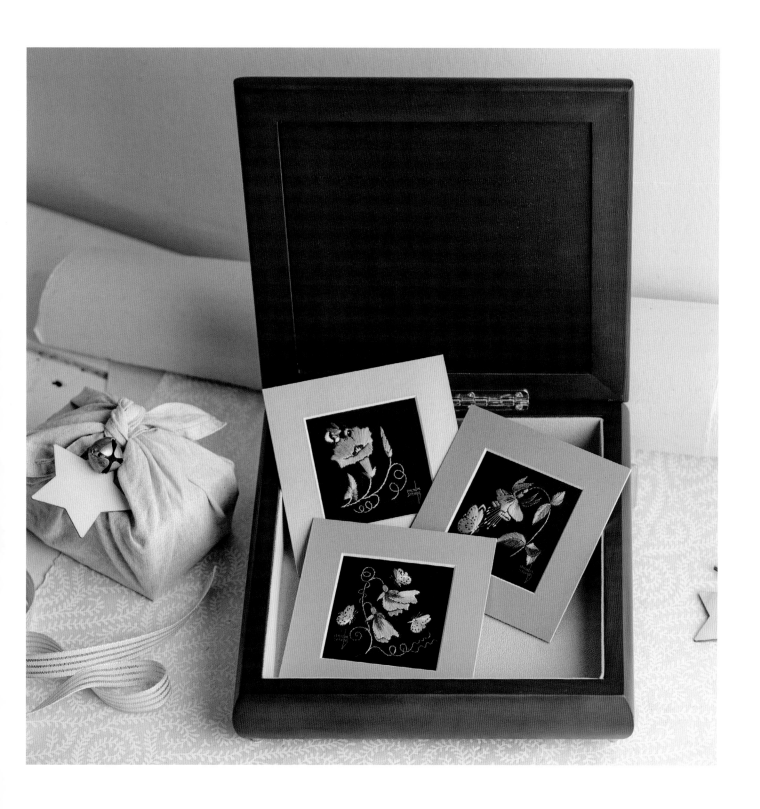

REQUIREMENTS

Fabric

35cm (14") square of pale yellow fine polycotton

15cm x 45cm wide (6" x 18") piece of black fine polycotton

Supplies

10cm (4") embroidery hoop with inner ring bound

28cm (11") embroidery hoop with inner ring bound

Sudberry House, Carol's Fancywork box wooden box with 19cm (7½") opening

22cm (8¾") square of firm card

3 x 10cm (4") squares of firm card

3 x 12.7cm (5") squares of gold mount board

Craft knife

Metal ruler

Masking tape

Lacing thread

Tracing paper

White or yellow dressmaker's carbon

Stylus or spent ballpoint pen

Fine black pen

Fine heat-soluble fabric marker

Sharp HB pencil

Needle

No. 10 crewel

Threads

Piper's Silks *silk floss*
A = black
B = new lettuce
C = champagne
D = white
E = pansy
F = deep purple
G = kingcup
H = deep crocus
I = crocus
J = dusky green
K = pale pink

L = pastel pink
M = pea green
N = conifer green
O = muscat
P = jade
Q = kingfisher green
R = China blue
S = ice blue
T = moss green
U = sycamore
V = light pansy

Piper's Silks *2/20 fine twisted silk*
W = black
X = white

Outline stitch, p215

Seed stitch, p215

Stem stitch, p215

Straight stitch, p215

this design uses

Outline stitch, p215

Seed stitch, p215

Stem stitch, p215

Straight stitch, p215

before you begin

See the liftout pattern for the embroidery designs

We recommend that you read the complete article

All embroidery is worked with THREE strands of thread unless specified

-----

PREPARATION FOR EMBROIDERY

Preparing the fabrics

Cut the piece of black polycotton into three, 15cm (6") squares. Neaten the edges of the pale yellow and black squares with a machine zigzag or overlock stitch to prevent fraying.

Transferring the design

Trace the large design and placement marks onto tracing paper with the black pen. Trace the three, small designs and placement marks onto tracing paper with the HB pencil.

Tape the large design to a lightbox or window. Centre the pale yellow polycotton over the design, aligning the placement marks with the straight grain, and trace the design using the fine, heat-soluble fabric marker. Place the fabric in the 28cm (11") hoop and tension until the surface is drum tight, taking care not to distort the design.

Place one square of black polycotton onto a smooth hard surface and centre one small design tracing over it, aligning the placement marks with the straight grain of the fabric. Pin the tracing in place at each top corner. Slide the dressmaker's carbon, chalk side down, between the fabric and the tracing. Pin in place at the centre of the lower edge. Using the stylus, re-trace the design, ensuring that you are pressing firmly enough to transfer the lines. Ensure all lines have been transferred before removing the carbon and tracing. Transfer the remaining small designs onto the remaining squares of black polycotton in the same manner.

Place one square of fabric in the 10cm (4") hoop and tension until the surface is drum tight.

BOX OF DELIGHTS

EMBROIDERY

Refer to the close-up photograph for colour and stitch placement.

All embroidery is worked in a hoop.

Order of work

Unless specified, all embroidery is worked with straight stitch using the photographs to determine the stitch direction.

SHADOW LINES

The shadow lines on the large design are worked first using two strands of **A**. These lines add depth and definition and are generally placed on the underside or one side of an element using stem, outline or straight stitch. Where there is no shadow line, separate elements by leaving a void between each.

> **HINT:** "Remember that the shadow line is a suggestion, rather than an inflexible rule, and so long as it broadly suggests the underside of each element, it does not have to conform exactly to the shown placement." **HELEN**

HELLEBORES

The showy, often speckled, 'petals' of a hellebore are actually sepals that serve to protect the flower. Over time, the smaller petals have developed into nectaries that produce nectar to attract the few insects that are active in the winter months when the plant flowers. They can number between five and twenty, are usually bright green and surround the pistils and stamens at the centre of the flower. The sepals change colour once the flower has been pollinated and remain surrounding the striking fruiting head until the seeds have matured. Flowering in winter, hellebores are commonly known as the 'Christmas Rose' in the northern hemisphere.

FLOWER 1

Centre

Stitch the teardrop-shaped carpels at the centre of the flower using **C**. Stitch the nectaries on each side of the carpels, radiating out from the centre, using **B**. Once the sepals have been stitched, work the filaments with long stitches using one strand of **C** and the anthers with seed stitch using two strands of **G**.

Sepals

Fill the inner surface of each white sepal using **D** then add long, spaced stitches at the base of each one using two strands of **V**. Fill the lower sepal with **V**, shading into **F** at the lower edge. Stitch the turnover on the right-hand petal using **V**.

FLOWER 2

Centre

Stitch the nectaries, radiating out from the centre, using **B**. Once the sepals have been stitched, work the filaments with long stitches using a single strand of **C**

and the anthers with seed stitch using two strands of **C**. Work several stamens in a similar manner using **B**.

Sepals

At the base of the left-hand sepals work a narrow area using **F** and fill the remaining area using **H**, leaving a void around the edge of the nectaries. Fill the remaining sepals using **H** and work the turnover at the upper edge of the top right-hand petal using **I**.

FLOWER 3

Centre

Fill the centre with radiating stitches using **J** and work the nectaries, radiating out from the centre, using **B**. Once the sepals have been stitched, work the filaments with long stitches using a single strand of **C** and the anthers with seed stitch using two strands of **G**.

Sepals

Work the base of each sepal using **I**, leaving a void around the nectaries, and fill the remaining area using **D**. Work long, spaced stitches over the lower half of each sepal using two strands of **E** for the lower left-hand sepal and two strands of **I** for the remaining sepals. Work the turnover on the two upper sepals using **K**.

FLOWER 4

Sepals

Work the inside of each sepal using **F** and the outside and small turnover on the lower left-hand sepal using **H**.

Stamens

Stitch the filaments using one strand of **C** and the anthers with seed stitch using two strands of the same thread.

FLOWER 5 AND BUD

Sepals

Stitch the outside of each sepal and the bud using **K** and the inside and small turnover on the right-hand sepal using **L**.

FLOWER 6

Sepals

Work the outside of each sepal using **I** and the inside using **H**.

FLOWER 7

Sepals

Stitch the outside of each sepal using **K** and the inside using **L**.

FLOWER 8

Sepals

Work in the same manner as Flower 7.

FLOWER 9

Sepals

Work in the same manner as Flower 6.

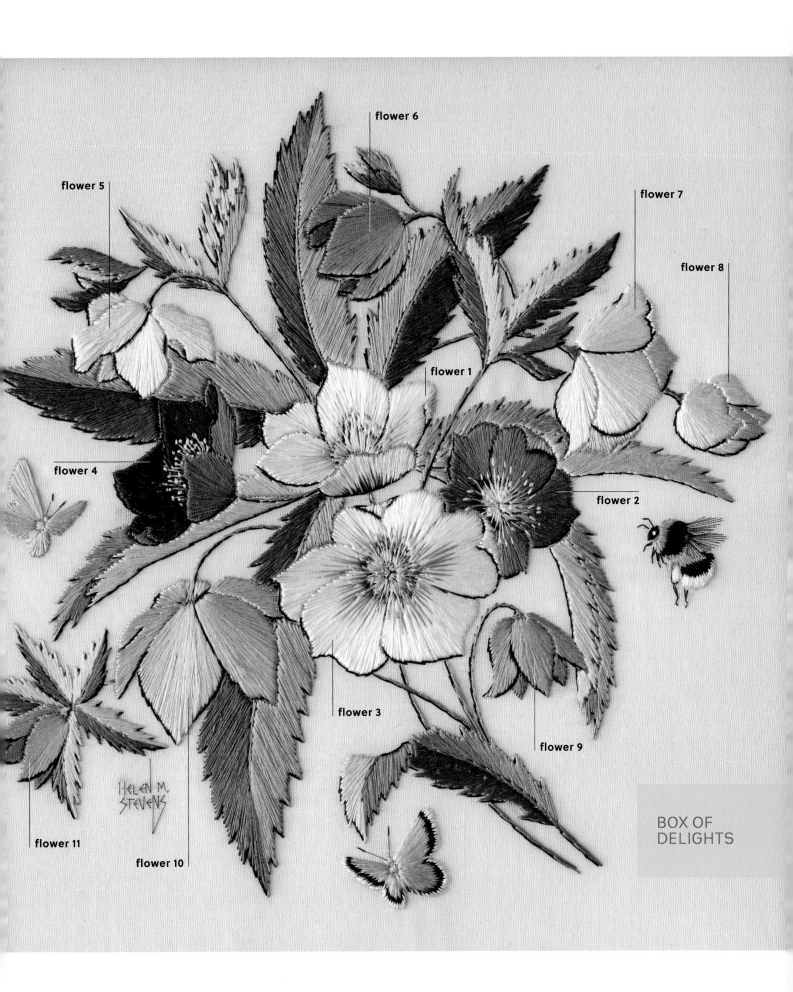

flower 6

flower 5

flower 7

flower 8

flower 1

flower 4

flower 2

flower 3

flower 9

flower 11

flower 10

HELEN M. STEVENS

BOX OF
DELIGHTS

FLOWER 10

Sepals

Fill each sepal using **L**. At the base of each sepal, work spaced stitches using **B** over the previous stitching.

FLOWER 11

Sepals

Work in the same manner as Flower 6.

FOLIAGE

Stems and leaf veins

Stitch the stems and leaf veins with stem stitch and outline stitch using **J**.

Smaller leaves

Using the photograph as a guide to colour placement, stitch the small leaves and medium leaf at the base of the design using combinations of **J**, **M**, **N** and **O**.

Larger leaves

Work the three lighter leaves radiating out from the centre of the design using **P**, **Q** and **U** and the four darker leaves using **P** and **Q**.

SMALL BLUE BUTTERFLY

Wings

Stitch the wings using **R**, radiating the stitches out from the thorax.

Body

Stitch the head, thorax and abdomen using **S** and the antennae using one strand of **W**, working three small stitches at the tip of each stalk.

HOLLY BLUE BUTTERFLY

Wings

Stitch the inner section of the wings using **R**, radiating the stitches out from the body. Stitch the inner band along the edge of the wings using **A** and the outer band using **D**.

Body

Stitch the head, thorax and abdomen using **S** and the antennae using one strand of **W**, working three small stitches at the tip of each stalk.

BEE

Wings

Work the wings using one strand of **W**, radiating the spaced stitches from the base of each wing.

Body

Using two strands of **C** and one strand of **G** together in the needle, work the pollen sack at the top of the hind leg. Stitch the head using **A**, the thorax using **G** then **A**, and the abdomen using **G**, **A** then **D**. Stitch the legs and antennae using one strand of **A** and the eye with a seed stitch using **D**.

SMALL DELIGHTS

SWEET PEA

Stems and tendrils

Using **T**, work the stems and tendrils with stem and outline stitch, beginning with a single strand at each tendril tip, increasing to two strands then three strands where the tendril meets the stem. Stitch the stems using **T**.

Flowers

Work the receptacle using **T** and the sepals using **P** and **Q**. Fill the lighter petals with **K** and the darker petals using **L**. Work stitches using **H** over the base of the lighter petals.

Butterflies

Each butterfly is worked in the same manner.

Work the underside of each wing using **C**, leaving a void between each wing. Stitch the wing markings with seed stitch using **A**, working perpendicular to the previous stitching. Fill the upper surface of each wing using **R**. Work several stitches at the base of each wing using **S**. Stitch the head, thorax and abdomen using the same colour. Work the antennae and legs using one strand of **X**, working three small stitches at the tip of each stalk.

FUCHSIA

Stems and leaves

Stitch the stem and leaf veins with stem stitch using **J**.

Fill one half of each leaf with **B** and the second half using **N**.

Flower

Work the ovary using **J** and the tube and sepals using **H**. Stitch the petals using **L** for the outer surface and **I** for the inner surface. Work stitches over the base of each petal using **F**. Stitch the stamens using one strand of **B** for the filaments and seed stitch and **D** for the anthers. Work the pistil using **L** for the style and **H** for the stigma.

Butterfly

Stitch the underside of the wings using **S** and the upper surface using **R** for the large area and **A** and **D** for the outer bands. Stitch the markings on the underside of the wings with seed stitch using **A**, working perpendicular to the previous stitching. Work the head thorax and abdomen using **S** and the antennae and legs using one strand of **X**, working three small stitches at the tip of each stalk.

MORNING GLORY

Stems, tendrils and leaf

Using **T**, stitch the stems, tendrils and leaf veins using stem and outline stitch, working the tendrils in a similar manner to the sweet pea. Fill the leaf using **O** and **T**.

Flower

Stitch the sepals using the same threads as the leaf. Fill the throat of the flower using **F** and the remaining area using **I**. Work the stamens with seed stitch using **C**. Stitch the bud using **I**.

Bee

Work the wings using one strand of **X**, radiating the spaced stitches from the base of each wing. Using two strands of **C** and one strand of **G** together in the needle, work the pollen sack at the top of the hind leg. Stitch the head using **A**, the thorax using **G** then **A**, and the abdomen using **G**, **A** then **D**. Stitch the legs and antennae using one strand of **A** and the eye with a seed stitch using **D**. Work highlights along the upper edge of the thorax using one strand of **X**.

CONSTRUCTION

Preparing the embroidered fabric

Remove any visible design lines from the large design using a hair dryer. Press, if necessary, face down into a soft, padded surface. Lace the embroidery over the 22cm (8¾") square of firm card, taking care to ensure that the design is centred.

Lace each small design over a 10cm (4") square of firm card.

Finishing the large design

Place the embroidery in the box opening and secure the backing.

Finishing the small designs

Cut a 7.5cm (3") square opening at the centre of each square of gold mount board using the craft knife and metal ruler.

Centre each small laced design behind a gold mount and tape securely in place using the masking tape.

SECRETS
BY
LAURENCE
LIEBLICH

OVERVIEW

Designer:	Project:	Technique:
Laurence Lieblich	Decorative box	Surface embroidery
Country of Origin:	**Fabric:**	**Threads:**
Switzerland	Linen	Stranded silk, metallic threads and crystals

Dimensions:
11.5cm x 10cm wide (4½" x 4")

Design Transfer Required: YES ☒   NO ☐

DESCRIPTION

A decorative box with shaped sides that tie at the top with silk ribbons to form a container for a Christmas surprise.

DESIGN NOTES

Avoiding the obvious red and green usually associated with Christmas, a striking palette of turquoise, copper and caramel silk is used to stitch the sinuous shapes that form the elegant design on each box side panel.

TECHNIQUE NOTES

Lustrous stranded silk threads are used to work the teardrop and foliate shapes using satin stitch, stem stitch and Palestrina stitch. Sparkling snowflakes are embroidered with fly stitch using metallic threads and a crystal is attached to the centre of each one. Each box side is carefully constructed with a silk ribbon tie at the top then all sides are attached to the square base to create the container.

Boxing Day

Originating in England in the early 19th century and celebrated with a Public Holiday in many Commonwealth countries, Boxing Day occurs on December 26th each year. The name is thought by some to have come from the boxes of gifts that were given to servants on the day after Christmas although there is some conjecture that it may have come from the church alms boxes that collected donations to help the poor and were opened on the Feast of St. Stephen, celebrated on December 26th. During a time of quite draconian employment conditions, servants were required to work on Christmas Day but were given the following day off to celebrate and visit their family. In countries that celebrate Boxing Day it is often now when the post-Christmas sales begin.

FROM THE DESIGNER

"When I was asked to participate in this project, I initially had some doubts before realising that it would be a very interesting challenge. Why the hesitation? How can one be original and break new ground without falling into banality? After a few days of reflection, I finally found the inspiration to create a unique object, imbued with symbolism and aesthetics. A long time ago, during my formative years, I was trained at college to solve problems in spatial geometry. Those acquired skills still allow me to mentally visualise what I want to achieve, and when I start a project, it's already fully realised in my head. So, I hardly ever make preliminary sketches. However, it took me nearly three months to flesh out all the details to bring to life the design of this small box, which was intended to be a receptacle for messages of happiness and health exchanged during the holiday season. To avoid the monotony of traditional Christmas colours, I chose cooler and purer shades, reminiscent of sunny winter mornings. The embroidered tree on the work is adorned with snowflakes, in a minimalist yet elegant setting. However, the real challenge was not the search for aesthetics, but rather the creation of a solid and functional structure. What caused me the most trouble until the final moments of this realisation was whether the structure that I had imagined, a bit like an origami, would take the correct final shapes. What a relief when I gathered the four faces of the box and attached them with ribbon and saw what I had envisioned come to life. Beyond the technical complexity of creating such an object, designing a piece of traditional embroidery is also a kind of tribute to craftsmanship and an age-old tradition that continues to fascinate and inspire creators around the world. It is thus participating in the transmission of precious know-how, but also in the preservation of a cultural heritage that has been entrusted to us so that we can transmit it in our turn. That is why I am convinced that this unpretentious object will be a source of happiness for the person who has the chance to receive it, and also for all those who have had the pleasure of creating it. So do not hesitate any longer, let yourself be tempted by this entertaining creation, and let your imagination come to life in space."

COLOUR PALETTE

SECRETS

REQUIREMENTS

Fabrics

40cm x 55cm wide (16" x 22") piece of cream linen

40cm x 55cm wide (16" x 22") piece of turquoise cotton

Supplies

15cm (6") embroidery hoop

8cm x 16cm wide (3⅛" x 6¼") piece of interlining

8cm (3⅛") square of thin wadding

8cm (3⅛") square of medium wadding

15cm (6") square of thin firm card

Cream sewing thread

Contrasting sewing thread

A4 sheet of white paper

Pins

Ruler

Craft glue

Tracing paper

Fine black pen

Fine heat-soluble fabric marker

Needles

No. 22 chenille
No. 7 crewel
No. 10 crewel

Threads, Ribbon & Beads

Au Ver à Soie metallic *tressé 4*
A = 021 copper
B = 2933 turquoise

Au Ver à Soie metallic *tressé 8*
C = 021 copper

Au Ver à Soie, soie d'Alger stranded silk
D = 132 vy lt turquoise
E = 133 lt turquoise
F = 4513 doe brown (2 skeins)
G = 4541 vy lt caramel
H = 4542 lt caramel (2 skeins)

House of Embroidery 7mm silk ribbon
I = 41 winter – 1m (40")

Swarovski 4mm xirius lochrose
J = crystal golden shadow

Swarovski 5mm xirius lochrose
K = crystal golden shadow

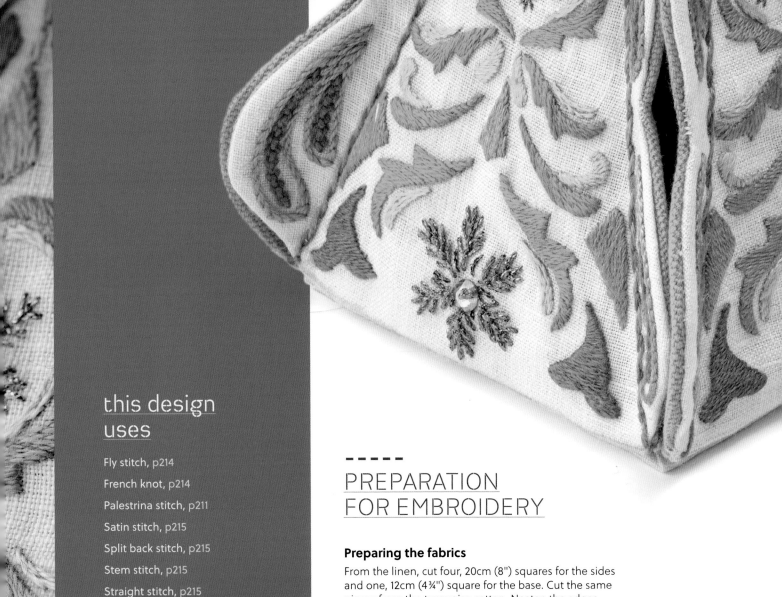

this design uses

Fly stitch, p214

French knot, p214

Palestrina stitch, p211

Satin stitch, p215

Split back stitch, p215

Stem stitch, p215

Straight stitch, p215

Whipped running stitch, p213

before you begin

See the liftout pattern for the embroidery design

We recommend that you read the complete article

All embroidery is worked with ONE strand of thread unless specified

PREPARATION FOR EMBROIDERY

Preparing the fabrics

From the linen, cut four, 20cm (8") squares for the sides and one, 12cm (4¾") square for the base. Cut the same pieces from the turquoise cotton. Neaten the edges of each 20cm (8") square with a machine zigzag or overlock stitch to prevent fraying.

Transferring the design

Using the black pen, transfer the embroidery design, triangle and placement marks onto tracing paper.

Tape the tracing to a lightbox or window. Centre one linen square over the tracing, aligning the placement marks with the straight grain and tape in place. Transfer the embroidery design to the linen using the fine, heat-soluble fabric marker. Using contrasting sewing thread, tack along each side of the triangle. Repeat on the remaining three squares of linen. Place one square into the 15cm (6") hoop and tension until the surface is taut, taking care not to distort the design. Once the embroidery on the first square is complete, remove the fabric from the hoop and replace with another square.

SECRETS

EMBROIDERY

Refer to the close-up photograph for colour placement.

Use the no. 22 chenille needle for the metallic threads, the no. 7 crewel needle for two or three strands of silk and the no. 10 crewel for one strand of silk.

All embroidery is worked in the hoop.

Order of work

Work each of the four sides in the same manner.

SNOWFLAKES

Small

Using **A**, work each snowflake arm with fly stitch, beginning with a straight stitch at the tip. Add a straight stitch between each arm using **B**. Attach a **J** crystal at the centre with a French knot using **A**.

Large

Using **C**, work each snowflake arm with fly stitch, beginning with a straight stitch at the tip. Add a straight stitch between each arm using **B**. Attach a **K** crystal at the centre with a French knot using **A**.

MOTIFS

Motif 1

Outline the upper and lower shapes with split back stitch and cover with satin stitch using **G**.

Stitch the side shapes in a similar manner using **F**.

Motif 2

Outline the large upper shapes with split back stitch and cover with satin stitch using **E**. Fill the small motifs with rows of stem stitch using **D**.

Motif 3

Outline the four large shapes with split back stitch and cover with satin stitch using **E**. Work the four small shapes with rows of stem stitch and the two teardrops at the centre with satin stitch using **D**.

Motif 4

Outline the four large shapes with split back stitch and cover with satin stitch using **E**. Work the two small upper shapes using **D** and the centre shape using **G** in a similar manner. Stitch the two small lower shapes with rows of stem stitch using **D**.

Motif 5

Outline the upper motif on each side with split back stitch and cover with satin stitch using **H**. Work the lower motif on each side in a similar manner using **F**.

Side motifs

Outline the teardrop shape on each motif with stem stitch using two strands of **H** and work the centre line on each one with Palestrina stitch using three strands of **F**.

SECRETS

- ● *Side motifs*
- ● *Motif 3*
- ● *Motif 1*
- ● *Motif 4*
- ● *Motif 2*
- ● *Motif 5*

CONSTRUCTION

All seam allowances are 1cm (⅜") unless otherwise specified. The shaded areas on the following diagrams indicate the right side of the fabric.

Preparing the side shaping

Transfer the shaping for the side panels onto the thin, firm card and cut into three pieces, the centre triangle and the two, scalloped side pieces (diag 1).

Preparing the embroidery

Remove the last square from the embroidery hoop, mist each panel lightly with water and press, face down, into a soft, smooth surface. Position the card triangle over the tacked triangle on each piece to check for any distortion and adjust the tacking if necessary.

On the wrong side of one embroidered panel, position the scalloped side pieces of card over the linen, aligning the long, straight edge of each one with the long, straight side of the triangle. Using the fine, heat-soluble fabric marker, trace around the scalloped edge of the side pieces to mark the shaping onto the linen (diag 2).

WRONG SIDE

Tack along the shaping using contrasting sewing thread.

Repeat on the remaining three pieces of linen.

Attaching the ribbon

Cut the length of **l** into four, 25cm (10") pieces. On the right side of one embroidered panel, position the end of one piece of ribbon at the apex of the triangle with 1cm (⅜") extending past the apex and pin in place (diag 3).

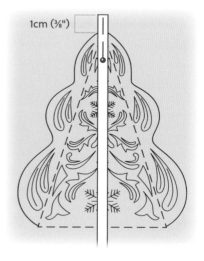

1cm (⅜")

Using the cream sewing thread, stitch the ribbon in place across its width at the apex of the triangle.

Repeat with the remaining panels and pieces of ribbon.

Attaching the lining

Position one square of turquoise cotton, wrong side uppermost, over one piece of linen, matching the edges and sandwiching the ribbon. Turn over so that the wrong side of the linen is uppermost and the shaping is visible. Pin the fabrics together close to the shaping.

Beginning on one side of the ribbon and using the cream sewing thread, back stitch the fabrics together down one scalloped edge, finishing at the lower corner of the triangle and removing the tacking as you work. Repeat on the second scalloped edge (diag 4).

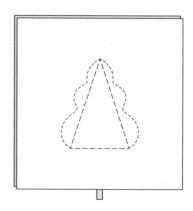

Cut out, leaving a 5mm (³⁄₁₆") seam allowance at the top, a 3mm (⅛") seam allowance down each side and a 2cm (¾") seam allowance at the base, taking care not to cut the ribbon (diag 5).

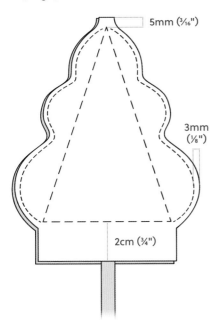

Clip the seam allowance where necessary and turn to the right side, ensuring that all fabric is turned out of the seams. Press carefully from the lining side. Using three strands of **F**, work running stitch down each long side of the triangle, working through both layers of fabric and removing the tacking as you work. Leave the tacking along the base of the triangle. Whip the running stitch using two strands of **H** on the linen side and two strands of **D** on the lining side.

Repeat with the remaining three panels.

Preparing the base

Cut the piece of interlining into two, 8cm (3⅛") squares. Place the 12cm (4¾") square of linen, wrong side uppermost, on a flat surface. Centre the 8cm (3⅛") square of thin wadding over the linen and one 8cm (3⅛") square of interlining over the wadding. Fold in each side of the linen over the interlining and glue or stitch in place (diag 6).

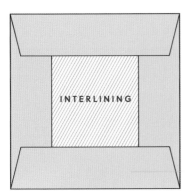

Allow to dry.

Repeat with the 12cm (4¾") square of turquoise cotton, the 8cm (3⅛") square of medium wadding and the remaining square of interlining.

Assembling the box

Place the linen base, wrong side uppermost, on a flat surface. With the lining side uppermost, position the lower seam allowance of one side panel over one side of the base, aligning the tacking along the lower edge of the linen triangle with one edge of the square and glue or stitch in place. Allow to dry. Remove the tacking along the base of the triangle. Repeat with the remaining three side panels. With the right side of the lining base uppermost and aligning the edges of the linen and lining squares, glue or stitch the lining base in place, sandwiching the seam allowance of the sides (diag 7).

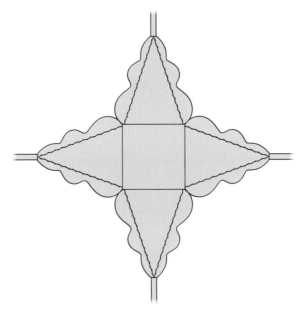

Allow to dry.

Finishing

Trim the end of each ribbon at an angle to prevent fraying.

Fold each side up and tie together at the top with the silk ribbons.

CHRISTMAS CHEER BY KATHERINE DIUGUID

OVERVIEW

Designer:	Project:	Technique
Katherine Diuguid	Hanging ornament with Christmas tree	Metal thread and bead embroidery
Country of Origin	**Fabric:**	**Threads:**
USA	Linen	Metal purl, metallic & beading thread and beads

Dimensions:	Design Transfer Required: YES [X] NO [ ]
10cm (4") in diameter	

- - - - -

DESCRIPTION

A hanging ornament featuring a Christmas tree worked with metal purl and a selection of glass beads and crystals.

- - - - -

DESIGN NOTES

A richly decorated Christmas tree sits at the centre of a circular ornament, held with a red ribbon loop. Metal threads combine with glass beads to create a colourful, highly textured surface.

- - - - -

TECHNIQUE NOTES

The embroidery and beading are worked onto a background of linen woven with a lurex thread, adding extra sparkle. Loops of green purl are used to create the tree branches and the trunk is stitched with metallic thread. Strings of bead 'lights' adorn the branches and decorations are added with larger beads. Loops of seed beads decorate the outer edge.

The Christmas Tree

The modern Christmas tree is thought to have its origins in 16th century Germany where a fir tree was brought into the home on December 24th and decorated with apples to become a 'paradise tree', part of the celebration of the feast day of Adam and Eve. German immigrants took this tradition to North America in the 17th century and it was introduced to England in the 19th century by Prince Albert, husband of Queen Victoria. Decorations became more ornate with candles added and blown glass ornaments, manufactured in Germany and Bohemia, could be purchased from around 1870. By 1890 strings of colourful, electric lights became available and the first artificial trees were produced in the 1930s.

FROM THE DESIGNER

"Growing up, my mother had a green ceramic Christmas tree that she would bring out yearly for the holidays. I loved taking the time to place all the peg lights in each of the holes and then watching it come to life with the flick of the switch. I cannot explain why this specific decoration brought me so much joy, but it did year after year. As the holidays approached while we were still in lockdown, I wanted to stitch something that simply brought joy. My mother's ceramic Christmas tree came to mind. I stitched a Christmas tree mixing metal embroidery and beading, full of texture and brimming with holiday cheer. I wanted it to sparkle like the memories of the tree that inspired it. This ornament is a scaled-down version of my original tree made with beaded edging for additional sparkle. I hope this project helps spread joy to everyone who stitches it and enjoys its decoration."

COLOUR PALETTE

CHRISTMAS
CHEER

REQUIREMENTS

Fabric

15cm (6") square of metallic natural linen

15cm (6") square of white cotton

Supplies

10cm (4") square of red wool felt

10cm (4") embroidery hoop

10cm (4") square of thin wadding

10cm (4") square of firm card

20cm x 6mm wide (8" x ¼") piece of red satin ribbon

Cutting pad

Goldwork scissors

Beeswax

Mellor

Silk pins

Tissue paper

Fine sepia marker with archival ink

Needle

No. 10 crewel

Threads & Beads

Au Papillon Fil d'Or Deluxe *metallic thread*
A = black gold

Gütermann *sewing thread*
B = 156 scarlet
C = 745 pepper green

Nymo *size B beading thread*
D = cream

METAL THREADS
E = green purl – 1m (40")
F = gilt bright check no. 6 – 10cm (4")
G = gilt super pearl purl – 5cm (2")

BEADS
H = assorted large beads and crystals
I = assorted seed and *Delica* beads

this design uses

Back stitch, p214

Beading, p214

Chipping, p207

Couching, p214

Stem stitch, p215

before you begin

See the liftout pattern for the embroidery design and circle template

We recommend that you read the complete article

All embroidery is worked with ONE strand of thread unless specified

-----

PREPARATION FOR EMBROIDERY

Preparing the fabrics

Neaten the squares of linen and cotton with a machine zigzag or overlock stitch to prevent fraying. Aligning the edges, place the linen over the cotton and place both fabrics in the 10cm (4") hoop, tensioning until they are drum tight.

Transferring the design

Using the template in the liftout pattern or a glass with the required diameter, mark a circle at the centre of the firm card and cut out.

Turn the hoop over so that the cotton is uppermost. Using the card circle as a template, mark the circle onto the cotton with the sepia marker. Tack around the marked line, through both layers of fabric, using **C**. Put the card circle aside for construction.

Using the sepia marker, mark the purl placement dots, tree trunk, circle and placement marks onto the tissue paper. Centre the design over the linen, aligning the placement marks with the straight grain and the circle with the line of tacking, and pin or tack securely in place. Using **C**, mark each dot with a small tacking stitch and the sides and base of the trunk with running stitch. Score the tissue paper and carefully tear away.

EMBROIDERY

Refer to the close-up photograph for colour placement. All embroidery is worked in the hoop.

Order of work

TRUNK

Outline the sides and lower edge with stem stitch and fill with tightly packed, vertical rows of stem stitch using **A**. Remove any visible tacking.

FOLIAGE

Using the goldwork scissors and cutting pad, cut the length of **E** into approximately 2cm–2.5cm (¾"–1") lengths. Vary the lengths so that the loops will not all be the same size. Bring a doubled, waxed length of **C** to the surface on the right-hand mark on the lower edge of the tree. Thread on a length of **E** and slide to the base of the thread. Take the needle to the back close to where it emerged to form a loop. Pull the thread until both ends of the purl are resting on the fabric. Do not pull too tightly. Lay the loop flat on the fabric and couch in place over the centre of the lower edge with a single stitch, taking care not to pull too tightly. Work a small back stitch beneath the purl to secure the thread. Do not trim away the thread. Stitch a purl loop at each mark in the same manner using the same thread.

LIGHTS

Work each swag of lights by bringing a doubled length of **D** to the surface at the desired position for one end of the swag. Thread on the required number of **I** beads, taking care to ensure that there are enough that the line will form a soft loop rather than sitting straight. Take the thread to the back at the desired position. Work a small back stitch beneath the swag to secure the thread. Do not trim away the thread. Work the required number of swags in the same manner using the same thread.

ORNAMENTS

Attach each large bead and crystal (**H**) individually using a doubled length of **D**.

STAR

Stretch the length of **G** the desired amount. Trim away the unstretched ends. Position one end of the pearl purl vertically at the top of the tree and couch between the second and third coils using **D**. Couch between the first and second coils twice. Trim the length to 13mm (½"), taking care to ensure that the cut end is facing the fabric, and couch between each coil to the end, stitching twice between the last two coils. Couch a shorter length of **G** over the centre of the first piece and perpendicular to it in the same manner. Couch two more pieces diagonally between the vertical and horizontal lengths in the same manner to create an eight-point star.

Using the goldwork scissors and cutting pad, cut chips of **F** the same length that the bright check is wide. Using a waxed length of **D**, attach a chip at each point of the star. Add additional chips radiating out from the star as desired.

- - - - -

CONSTRUCTION

All seam allowances are 1.5cm (⅝"). The shaded areas on the following diagrams indicate the right side of the fabric.

Preparing the embroidered fabric

Remove the embroidery from the hoop and, leaving a 1.5cm (⅝") seam allowance from the line of tacking, cut out. Using strong thread and leaving a tail at each end, work a line of gathering 7mm (⁵⁄₁₆") in from the raw edge.

Preparing the card, felt and wadding

Using the card circle as a template, mark and cut a circle from the red wool felt and the thin wadding. Trim 2mm (¹⁄₁₆") from around the wadding circle and 1mm (¹⁄₃₂") from around the felt circle.

Assembling the ornament

Centre the wadding circle on one side of the card circle and position the card, wadding side down, over the back of the embroidery, aligning the edge of the card with the tacked circle. Pull up the gathering threads firmly and tie off securely. Lace the seam allowance firmly over the card (diag 1).

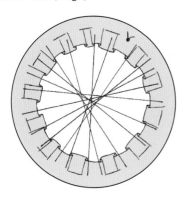

Adding the hanging loop and backing

Remove the tacking marking the circle. Fold the length of red ribbon in half and stitch 1cm (⅜") at the raw ends to the seam allowance at the top of the circle using **B** (diag 2).

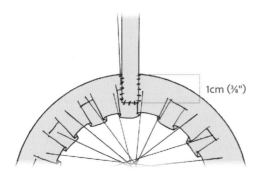

1cm (⅜")

Position the red wool felt circle over the back of the card and stitch in place around the edge of the circle using the same thread.

Working the beaded edge

Secure a length of **D** at the edge of the circle and thread on eight, **I** beads. Take a small stitch into the circle 6mm (¼") along the edge and go back up through the last bead. Thread on seven, **I** beads and take a small stitch through the circle 6mm (¼") along the edge and go back up through the last bead. Continue working in this manner around the circle. When working the last loop, thread on only six beads and take the needle down through the first bead of the first loop and secure the thread.

CHRISTMAS
CHEER

STITCH GLOSSARY

BEADED
PICOT CHAIN
STITCH

This stitch creates a sparkling, decorative border. Here, the picot chains create the appearance of tiny flower buds and leaves connected in a row.

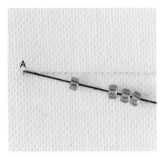

1 Emerge at A. Thread on one pink and three green beads.

2 Take the thread back through the pink bead, forming a chain. Take the needle to the back at A.

3 Holding the chain flat, emerge at B. Take the thread down through the centre green bead and to the back at B.

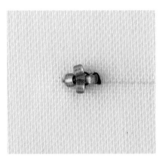

4 Pull the thread through, ensuring the beads sit in a diamond.

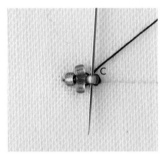

5 Emerge at C, above the centre green bead. Take the needle down through the bead.

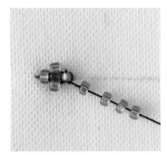

6 Pull the thread through. Thread on one pink and three green beads.

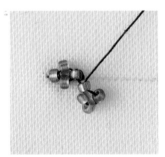

7 Take the thread back through the pink bead, pulling the beads into a chain.

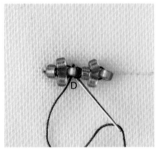

8 Take the thread down through the anchored green bead of the previous chain and to the back at D.

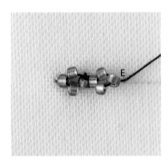

9 Emerge at E, beside the centre green bead of the new chain.

10 Repeat steps 3–9 to the end of the row. Anchor the last chain following step 3.

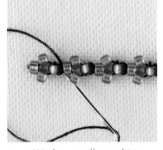

11 Work a small couching stitch over the thread between two picot chains.

12 Pull the thread through so that it disappears between the beads. Repeat along the row.

BEADED PICOT EDGING

This beaded lace edging creates a colourful finish along the folded edge of a hem. The spacing indicated is for size 15 seed beads.

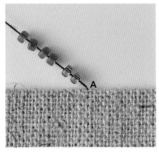

1 Emerge through the fold at A. Pick up two green and four red beads.

2 Go down through the lowest red bead, pull the thread through and pick up two green beads.

3 Take a stitch through the fold from B, 3mm (⅛") from A, to C, a further 3mm (⅛") from B. Pull the thread through.

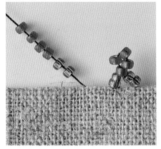

4 Pick up two green and four red beads.

5 Go down through the lowest red bead of the group and pick up one green bead.

6 Go down through the lowest green bead at B and pull the thread through.

7 Take the needle through the fold from B to C and emerge through the lowest green bead.

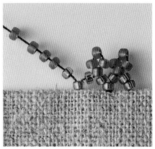

8 Pick up one green and four red beads.

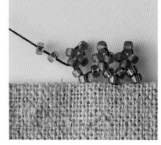

9 Go down through the lowest red bead of the group, pull the thread through and pick up two green beads.

10 Circular hem. Repeat steps 3–9 until there is space for one last picot.

11 Pick up beads as required to form the picot and pick up one green bead.

12 Go down through the lowest green bead and the hem at A. Pull the thread through.

BINDING A TASSEL NECK

This method cleverly conceals the ends of the cord.

1 Leaving a short tail along the head of the tassel, loop the binding cord over the neck area as shown.

2 Working from the top downwards, wrap the neck of the tassel for the desired length, leaving the upper end of the short tail and the loop uncovered.

3 Take the wrapping cord through the loop, pulling it taut.

4 Pull the short tail firmly upwards, closing the loop.

5 Continue to pull firmly so that the end of the loop is drawn up beneath the wraps.

6 Trim each end of the binding cord as close to the wrapping as possible.

BRICK STITCH

Brick stitch creates a firm, bead edge. Using a long length of thread, begin with a double knot and emerge near the edge on the front. Hide the knot between the layers.

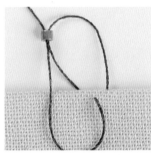

1 String on a bead. Take the needle through both layers from the back to the front. Go back up through the bead.

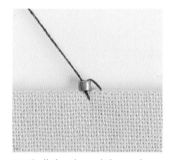

2 Pull the thread through and bring the bead down to the edge.

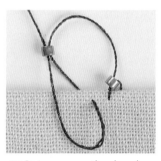

3 String on another bead. Take the needle through both layers from the back to the front. Take the thread back up through the bead.

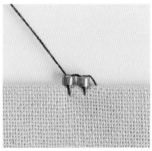

4 Pull the thread through and bring the bead down to the edge.

5 Repeat steps 3–4 to complete the row. Secure the thread with tiny stitches near the edge.

CHIPPING

This type of filling is worked using very short lengths of cut purl, called 'chips', stitched in place close together to cover a shape. Check purl is most often used for this technique because the texture of the thread is much more effective than smooth purl.

1 Using a padded cutting board, cut the check purl into short lengths, each as long as they are wide.

2 Secure the thread and bring it to the front within the shape. Thread a chip onto the needle and slide it to the base of the thread.

3 Lay the chip on the fabric and take the needle to the back at the opposite end of the chip.

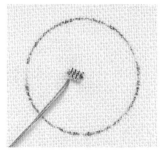

4 Bring the thread to the front next to the first chip.

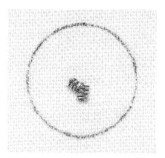

5 Stitch a second chip in place close to the first in the same manner as before, but in a different direction.

6 Continue to stitch the chips in place close together and in random directions to fill the shape.

CUTTING OUT A WIRED SHAPE

When detached shapes are added to a ground fabric, the wire tails are inserted through the fabric and secured to the wrong side of the work.

1 Complete the stitching following the instructions.

2 Maintaining tension on the fabric, cut out, angling the blades of the scissors as close as possible under the blanket stitch edge.

3 Scratch the edge of the shape to lift any short fabric tails.

4 Retrim as needed, working from the back of the shape.

5 Wired, detached shape ready for use.

DOT STITCH

This stitch is particularly effective when used next to satin stitch because of the contrast of textures. The stitches should always be worked as back stitches to maintain the correct tension on the thread, giving the stitches greater definition.

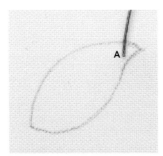

1 Bring the thread to the front at A.

2 Take the thread to the back at B and re-emerge at A.

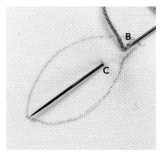

3 Take the thread to the back at B and emerge at C.

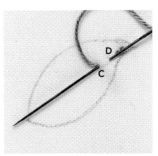

4 Take the thread to the back at D and re-emerge at C.

5 Continue working in this manner to the end of the row.

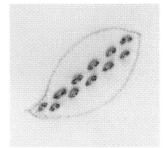

6 Turn the work 180 degrees. Work a second row in the same manner, offsetting the stitches.

7 Continue working rows, offsetting each one to the previous until the shape is filled.

DOUBLE RUNNING STITCH

Also known as Holbein stitch this is an effective way of creating a solid line of straight stitches.

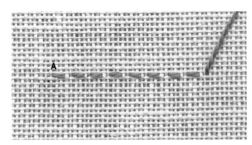

1 Bring the thread to the surface at A. Work running stitch along the line over and under two threads.

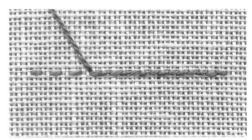

2 Work a second line of running stitches in the remaining spaces to create a solid line of stitching.

JOINING STITCH

Joining stitch is used to join panels neatly and evenly. Position the panels with edges and back stitches aligned.

1 Emerge at the right-hand end on the lower panel.

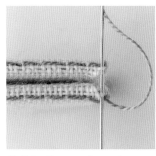

2 Take the needle under the linen thread on the opposite corner and the linen thread on the first corner, ensuring the fabric holes are aligned.

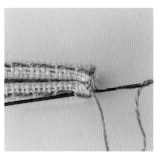

3 Pull the thread through. Slip the needle back through the same hole on the first panel and slide it behind the first back stitch.

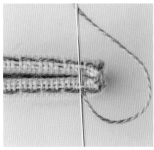

4 Pull the thread through. Take a stitch through the fold on each edge in the same manner as before, between the back stitches.

5 Pull the thread through and slip the needle to the end of the next back stitch.

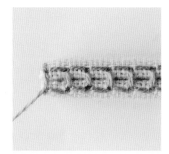

6 Repeat steps 4 and 5 to the end of the row.

NOTE: To begin a thread, tie a knot in the end. Take the needle through the linen, and pull the thread firmly until the knot 'pops' through the fabric to the wrong side.

To end a thread, tie a knot 6mm (¼") from the last stitch. Slip the needle back under the back stitches along the row just worked and emerge between two back stitches. Pull the thread through firmly until the knot 'pops' through the fabric. Maintaining tension on the thread, trim it close to the surface.

PADDED
SATIN STITCH

Filling a shape with satin stitch worked over padding creates a beautiful play of light and shadow over the smooth, raised surface. A few stitches are commonly used to create padding.

For a neat finish, it is helpful to create a stable edge by first outlining the shape with split stitch.

1 **Running stitch**. Beginning inside the outline, work running stitches that are long on the surface and very short on the back of the work around the shape.

2 Working inwards, fill the shape.

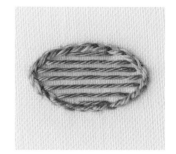

3 **Straight stitch**. Work spaced straight stitches across the shape.

4 **Stem stitch**. Beginning inside the outline, work stem stitch, only taking a small stitch back towards each previous stitch.

5 Working inwards, fill the shape with rounds of stem stitch.

6 **Chain stitch**. Beginning inside the outline, work chain stitch around the shape.

7 Working inwards, fill the shape with rounds of chain stitch.

8 **All padding**. When the padding is complete, change to a new thread to work the satin stitch over the padding and outline.

PALESTRINA STITCH

Palestrina is a highly decorative linear stitch that is excellent for joins, edges and outlines. The knots should be evenly spaced.

1 Bring the thread to the front at A. Take the needle to the back at B and pull through.

2 Bring the thread to the front at C.

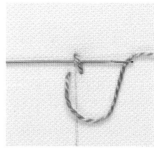

3 Slide the needle from right to left under the stitch.

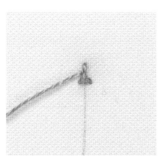

4 Pull the thread through until the loop lies snugly against the stitch.

5 Loop the thread and slide the needle as shown under the first stitch. Ensure that the loop is under the needle.

6 Pull the thread through to form a knot.

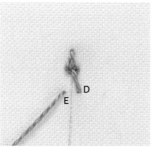

7 Take the needle to the back at D and emerge at E.

8 Slide the needle from right to left under the stitch.

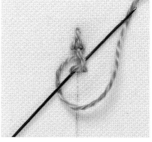

9 Pull the thread through. Loop the thread and slide the needle under the stitch as before.

10 Pull the thread through. Continue working stitches in the same manner.

SATIN STITCH DOT

This is a quick and effective way to stitch small padded shapes with a domed profile.

1 Work an outline around the shape using split stitch.

2 Work a star of crossed straight stitches at the centre of the shape.

3 Working within the outline, fill the shape with satin stitch.

4 Beginning at the centre and working perpendicular to the previous row, cover the outline and padding on one side with satin stitch.

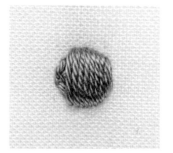

5 Return to the centre and fill the remaining side of the shape.

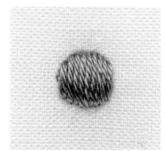

6 Completed satin stitch dot.

SINKING WIRE TAILS

To form a hole large enough to pass metal thread or wire tails through, use a needle with a large eye and sharp tip. Wire may show through the fabric, so ensure the tails are bent behind the detached element.

1 Insert the large needle into the fabric at the required position until the eye is halfway through.

2 Take the wire tails and any thread tail to the back through the eye of the needle and fabric.

3 Pull the needle all the way through the fabric and remove.

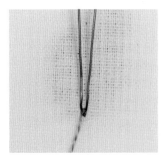

4 On the wrong side, pull the wire and thread through so that the base of the detached element is against the ground fabric. Bend the wire tails back against the fabric.

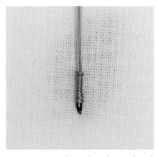

5 Using either the thread tail or a new thread, overcast the wire to the backing fabric only.

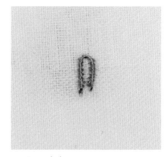

6 Bend the wire into a U. Stitch to secure and trim the wire tails.

7 Bend the detached shape into the required position.

TURNING CORNERS WITH PEARL PURL

When outlining angular shapes such as squares you should start and finish at one corner.

1 Couch the pearl purl in place along one side. Place the point of a mellor or an awl at the corner point. Bend the pearl purl around the point.

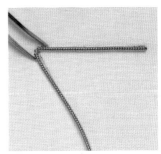

2 Taking care not to stretch the pearl purl, use tweezers to carefully pinch the point to the correct angle.

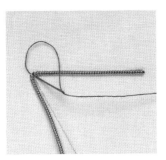

3 Bring the couching thread to the front outside the point. Place a stitch over the pearl purl.

4 Click the stitch down between the coils. Continue to stitch along the second side.

WHIPPED RUNNING STITCH

Work a line of running stitch. Use a tapestry needle for the whipping.

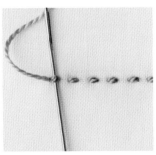

1 Emerge at the end of the line and slide the needle down beneath the first stitch.

2 Pull through. Slide the needle down beneath the next stitch.

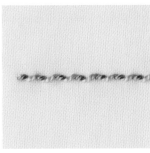

3 Repeat along the line. Take the thread to the back and secure.

BASIC STITCHES

Back Stitch

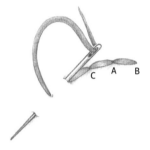

Beading

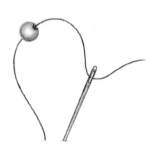

Blanket stitch

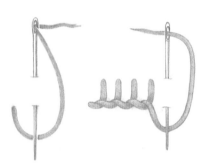

Couching

A laid thread is attached using a second thread.

Detached chain

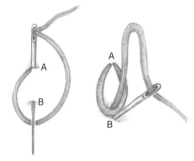

Fly Stitch

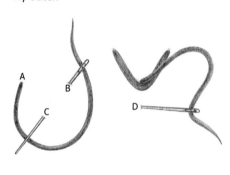

French Knot

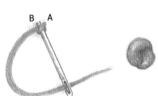

Long and short blanket stitch

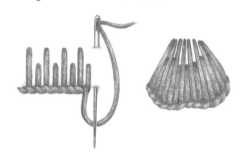

Ghiordes Knot

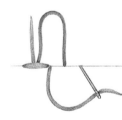

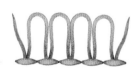

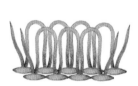

Long and short stitch

Outline stitch

The thread is always kept above the needle.

Overcasting

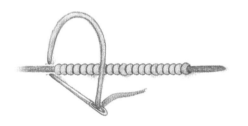

Satin Stitch

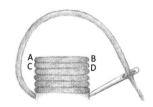

Seed stitch

Work as back stitches

Split back stitch

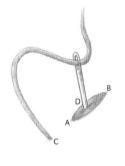

Split stitch

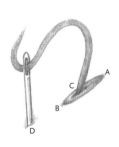

Stem stitch

The thread is always kept below the needle.

Straight stitch

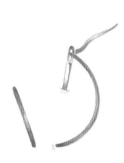

Trellis couching

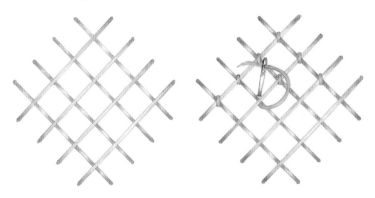

THE DESIGNERS

HAZEL BLOMKAMP

Author of several books, Hazel has become well known for her modern interpretation of crewel embroidery incorporating a wide range of stitches and needlework techniques not normally associated with this style. She lives in South Africa and has an extensive range of designs available on her website, along with online tuition for her signature techniques and selected projects.

TRISH BURR

Trish's threadpainted designs and her inviting style of instruction, developed over many years as a self-taught stitcher, have become internationally popular. She is the author of several books and regularly releases new patterns ranging from spectacular bird portraits to miniature designs.

KATHERINE DIUGUID

In addition to her love of goldwork and teaching embroidery, Katherine's current studio work investigates the magic of colour in stitch. She holds a master's degree in hand dressmaking and embroidery and certificates in stitched textiles from the Royal School of Needlework, City & Guilds UK, and Central Saint Martins.

NATALIE DUPUIS

Natalie holds a MEd and teaches and lectures internationally. She specializes in historic goldwork with specific interests in or nué and colour theory. Her work features regularly in *Inspirations* and *Piecework* magazines, and she is a needlework judge with the EGA. Natalie is from Ontario, has lived in Europe, and now resides in Montreal with her husband and two young children.

DI KIRCHNER

Di's real passion for needle and thread grew while working for over twenty years in a needlework store, where she designed and taught embroidery. Having completed the Royal School of Needlework's Certificate Course, she is now furthering her education through their Diploma in Technical Hand Embroidery, and continues to enjoy teaching a wide variety of embroidery techniques.

MARGARET LEE

Margaret learnt Chinese embroidery from a young age and is also an internationally accredited teacher of Traditional Japanese Embroidery and Japanese Bead Embroidery. Passionate about preserving the traditional arts of Japanese and Chinese embroidery, she has authored three books and the chapter on Embroidery for *The Routledge Encyclopedia* on *Traditional Chinese Culture*.

LAURENCE LIEBLICH

Laurence grew up in a very culturally rich environment, and even as a young girl, her artistic impulses turned to the art of embroidery. As a self-taught artist, she creates instinctively, allowing for a very free interpretation of her work. For many years she has run an embroidery studio in Switzerland, providing her with the opportunity to constantly share new ideas with her students. She also maintains a blog offering numerous projects for everyone to enjoy.

ANA MALLAH

A self-taught artist, Ana draws inspiration from anything pretty and flowers always seem to capture her interest the most. Passionate about embroidery, she particularly loves threadpainting and stumpwork. Ana works as an embroidery designer and teacher, and loves discussing stitches, threads and colours with like-minded people all day long.

BETSY MORGAN

Betsy has dabbled in every kind of needlework imaginable, but her first loves are counted thread and stumpwork. She has been designing and teaching needlework for twenty years and retired from teaching at the end of 2020. Now living in the Charleston, South Carolina area, Betsy enjoys sharing in the stitching community there, and has authored two books, *Willing Hands* and *Willing Hands 2*.

SUSAN O'CONNOR

Susan has devoted many years to exploring the world of embroidery. She has become renowned for her glorious botanical designs inspired by the Elizabethan period, worked with lustrous silk threads and gold paillettes. Susan teaches internationally, has authored two books and is the Editor of *Inspirations* magazine.

HELEN M. STEVENS

In 1981 Helen made embroidery both her career and her raison d'etre. International commissions, exhibitions, worldwide tours and twelve embroidery books followed. Her ability to capture the minutiae of nature gained her the accolade of being the first textile artist elected to the prestigious Society of Women Artists. In 2024 Helen celebrates 20 years of contributions to *Inspirations'* magazines and books.

DI VAN NIEKERK

Di is a professional fibre arts instructor, designer and author of fourteen best-selling books on needlecrafts. She heads the Dicraft team that creates her beautiful range of silk ribbons, panels and kits. She travels internationally to teach at festivals, conventions and shows, and shares useful information and inspirational stories on her blog with embroiderers all over the world.

KITS

THE NUTCRACKER

Page 6

A beloved Christmas decoration depicted in or nué with additional embellishments to enhance the design

Kit contains: Fabrics, wool felt, mount board, feathers, tissue paper, embroidery threads, paillettes and needles

A CHRISTMAS ROSE

Page 24

Ornament with a stumpwork hellebore and gold star worked over a background of counted thread embroidery

Kit contains: Fabrics, fusible interfacing, interlining, wire, card, embroidery threads and needles

A SPRIG OF HOLLY

Page 40

Elegant brooch with holly berries and leaves worked with silk threads

Kit contains: Fabric, wires, locking brooch pin, embroidery threads, beads and needle

PAT'S BONBON

Page 52

A bonbon to use every year, adorned with sparkling poinsettias, flowers and leaves in three-dimensional beading

Kit contains: Silk fabric, wool felt, zip, ribbon, dark green sewing thread, pipe, beading threads, beads and needle

A SUMMER CHRISTMAS

Page 72

Wreath with softly shaded hydrangeas and berries to honour the different seasons around the world at Christmas

Kit contains: Fabrics, wires, wool felt balls, embroidery threads, beads and needles

FOLK ART BIRD ORNAMENT

Page 90

Colourful bird with flowers and snowflakes inspired by Scandinavian folk art

Kit contains: Fabrics (inc. with pre-printed design), wool felt, card, ribbon, white sewing thread, embroidery threads, beads and needle

Inspirations
Ready-to-Stitch kits
are available at
inspirationsstudios.com

CHRISTMAS WREATH

Page 104

Wreath with Christmas reds and greens, framed in a hoop bound with hand-dyed silk ribbon

Kit contains: Fabrics, hoop, card, metal ring, white sewing thread, embroidery threads, ribbons, beads and needles

WHITE CHRISTMAS

Page 120

White hanging ornament with a garland of leaves, beaded berries and twigs

Kit contains: Fabric, wires, wooden beads, metal ring, bias binding, ribbon, embroidery threads, beads and needles

MEMORIES

Page 136

Centrepiece table mat sumptuously worked with Japanese-style bead embroidery

Kit contains: Fabric with pre-printed and hand-painted design, adhesive felt, adhesive vinyl, sewing threads, embroidery threads, beads and needles

BOX OF DELIGHTS

Page 154

Large design of hellebores and small designs of sweet pea, fuchsia and morning glory

Kit contains: Fabrics (inc. with pre-printed design), dressmaker's carbon, card, embroidery threads and needle

Note: Wooden box available separately

SECRETS

Page 172

Pyramid box with surface embroidery in silk and metallic threads

Kit contains: Fabrics, interlining, waddings, card, cream sewing thread, embroidery threads, ribbon, beads and needles

CHRISTMAS CHEER

Page 188

Sparkling Christmas tree ornament embellished with metal thread, beads and crystals

Kit contains: Fabrics, wool felt, wadding, card, ribbon, tissue paper, embroidery threads, beads and needle

ACKNOWLEDGEMENTS

A simple idea executed well is never easy.

The Design Collective was never a one-off. This project was always about creating a series of books that showcase needlework like never before – a singular idea presented twelve different ways.

After the release of our first volume, Pincushions, there was a sense of great excitement at what had been achieved, along with eager anticipation of what was yet to come.

For The Design Collective Volume 2, we decided to go all out and select one of the biggest events on the calendar to celebrate in stitch – Christmas.

With such an iconic and significant occasion to draw inspiration from, having received such favourable responses after briefing our team and the needlework artists, we knew we were onto something special.

Here is the roll call of the fabulous individuals who took an idea and, once again, executed it brilliantly...

Ana, Betsy, Di (Kirchner), Di (van Niekerk), Hazel, Helen, Katherine, Laurence, Margaret, Natalie, Susan & Trish, your collective vision and artistic expressions celebrating Christmas are nothing short of exceptional. Thank you for plying your talent and treasure for all to enjoy.

The brilliantly creative duo, Brendan & Natalie, brought each project to life through the lens of the camera. B&N your mark on this book, and indeed the series, is indelible and everlasting.

Putting this book series into the hands of our graphic designer is akin to working with a master chef. He collects all the ingredients, preps each element and whirs away in the kitchen until, as if by magic, he emerges with a masterpiece. Lynton, you are truly a design guru.

Then there is all the heavy lifting. From step-by-step tutorials, detailed instructions, proofing, coordination of myriad elements, kit sourcing, schedule management, promotional materials... the list goes on. Susan, Ellaine, Jessie, Sue and Willow, your commitment, skill and fervour are beyond compare and worthy of the highest recognition.

Finally, we have the great privilege of handing the finished product over to you, our devoted needlework community. You take this kernel of inspiration, a book full of ideas and possibilities, make them your own and spread the joy of needlework one stitch at a time, each in your own way. Thank you for joining us in all we do.

Long may needlework be the elixir of life.

KRISTIAN & ANDREA FLEMING

Owners & Custodians | Inspirations Studios